A Me[mory of]
Love, Hate &
Hope

This is Angela's story

Angela Decosta

This is a true story of Love , Hate, Sadness and survival

Intro.

1960's Derby.

The sixties was a decade of revolution in politics, in the music architecture and in fashion. There was the Beatles, Miniskirts, Psychedelic colors in the homes and clothes. There were the Mods and Rockers, Teddy boys not forgetting the Hippies. The latest hair style included the Beehive a must have. It was also the year that Angela Evelyn Scaife was born 10th November 1962 in the local Women's Hospital. Born to Pauline and George Scaife who can only be described as none doting parents.

Angela was the first born daughter after four elder brothers .Apparently father always wanted a girl but has you will find out later in the book that she just wasn't what he wanted for some reason.

So like I said there were four older brothers all very close in age. After Angela another baby girl arrived followed by another boy another girl then finally another boy. They were all born close together. So yes there were nine children in all.

So you would think that there would be a close relationship between them but hell no there certainly were not close. It was more like they didn't like each other not even the Mother and Father.

There was arguments really nasty ones at that, and sometimes there was violence it was a very scary and frightening childhood. There didn't seem like a day went by without some sort of drama going on with someone.

Thursday through to Sunday I would say was the worse time. Thursday being pay day for the older brother who was working has a painter and decorator also attending Wilmorton College doing his apprentice. I do remember him coming home from work in his not so white overalls covered in paint. His hair was black and quite long also covered in white paint. He also grew up liking his pint of beer. But I think that Derby County Football was a love of his. He went to the home matches at the Derby Baseball Ground in the Normanton area of Derby .It was close to a pub called the Valucan Arms which is where I would imagine the Derby fans would go before the match.

Derby Football Club played at the Baseball Ground for over one hundred years before moving to Pride Park in Derby in 1997.

His other love was Reggie music, Bob Marley was his favourite though .You always knew when he was home because you could hear the music playing. So when he moved to Douglas Street in Derby with his then partner Julie he was happy that there was a Caribbean Club at the bottom of the road it was quite a big place at the time owned by the Douses. I remember him taking me there once it was quite dark inside, music playing so loud you couldn't hear yourself think. And to be honest you could get has high as a kite in there just by standing at the bar. It was buzzing.

David lived with his then partner Julie they had a beautiful baby girl named Donna I used to baby sit her. It was the highlight of my week. Every Friday after school I would run all the way from our house on Leopold St to his house not stopping till I reached there. It was my escape for the weekend away from all the arguments, fighting, chaos that occurred on weekends and all the madness.

I used to help Julie with the baby. I also remember taking all the washing to the local launderette in a big black bin liner I got it washed and dried then return with it all done. My best time was when I was allowed to take donna to the park it was the Arboretum based in the Rose Hill Street area it had been a wonderful park since 1840 founded by Joseph Strutt it was really nice.

Julie and I would often go food shopping on a Saturday which I loved because I knew we would eat and drink well.

I even got treated to sweets or chocolate. Some Saturdays Julies brother Joey would just turn up he was homeless quite ruff and dirty in his appearance and very quite. Julie always gave him something hot to eat and drink before he went on his way, Joey was harmless bless him.

It wasn't long before David and Julie had another baby this time a boy who they named luwin. I just loved being there. But sadly it wasn't to last has David and Julie eventually split up with Julie taking the children with her.

I only ever saw Julie by accident after that bumping into her in the town centre now and again.

David also went his own way and we grew apart not really seeing each other but that is what happened to us all once we were grown, apart from the odd one that keep in touch.

Has far as I know David now lives in the Mackworth area of Derby with his new family. I hope has been happy and I bet has still football mad.

Stuart

I always thought that my second elder brother Stuart had the right idea. He was born Stuart Owen scaife on the 25th July 1957. Somewhat more career minded. But the scaife trate was him in has well, yes he liked his beer.

But having said that he joined the Army Cadets at a young age oh boy he had his head screwed on right I'd say. He found a great way to free himself from the madhouse and all its madness. When he left school he went straight into the Army. He was well travelled but also saw and experienced a lot of awful things. He served in Northern Ireland where one of his friends was killed.

We used to write to each other on a regular bases but he was always telling me off for putting my name and address on the back of the envelope saying it was for security reasons. He made a lot of friends while he was in the Army. But I admit it I loved it when he came home on leave. On one such occasion he brought home his wife Caroline and their baby girl. He wasn't a well behaved person by any stretch of the imagination he was a rebel at times. But like I say I think he felt angry inside about a lot of things not having the doting parents who were proud of you hurt so much never being told they loved you has got to effect you no matter who or how strong you think you are.

After being in the Army and reaching Sergeant status he left the Army and moved back to Derby with Caroline and by then he had three girls all beautiful and cute.

But he found civilian life hard to cope with he seemed a different person .I think he had PTS but back then it wasn't a thing. He used to go drinking and always getting into a fight someone. Getting barred from pubs. It wasn't a surprise when Caroline left him taking the girls with her. He kept in touch with the girls and has they got older he used to go on a visit to see them.

After a while he seemed to settle down and calm down. He was actually my best man when I got married the first time. He was brilliant acting on my orders not to let father go to the pub before the wedding and to keep his eyes open for any trouble during the whole wedding which he managed to do God knows how but he did it.

Then he met and married Lesley he seemed to be happier than I had seen him for a long time. New wife new step children who took to him like a duck to water. He was contented now a lovely wife who loved him dearly, lovely home, family around him and of courses his friends. Not forgetting his beloved dog.

He and Lesley were married for over twenty years before it all came to a crashing end. On June 22nd 2017 Stuart suddenly passed away while on a Cruise with Lesley. It was a heart attack. A great bloody shock I wasn't expecting that phone call from my aunty Linda I couldn't believe it.

Lesley had to travel home all alone it must have felt for ever to get home God only knows what was going through her mind how she did it I' ll never know. He was taken far too soon.

It was a long time before the funeral could go ahead. Lesley had to sort out how to get him back home then organize the funeral.

But on the day we said our goodbyes Lesley had done him so proud. And to his daughter Stacey who helped carry him into the chapel so brave of her. It was heart breaking I tried to hold it together but couldn't especially when the Last Post was played.

So all that's left for me to say is G od bless sleep tight may you rest in peace brother.

Stuart Owen scaife

25-07-1957 – 22-06-1922.

Kevin

Third born to the non doting parents on the 12th December 1959. If I'm honest I can't really remember that much from when we were kids. I know he also had the Scaife trate yes you have guessed it the drink.

I know he used to work on the trains has a guard. He met and married a nurse Julie she was so lovely. I got on very well with her. They went onto have two girls Claire and Kathryn. Again I used to go to their house for a sleep over and help with the girls but has I got older I seemed to have drifted away. In the end though Kevin and Julie also went their separate ways with Julie taking the girls with her to live in Cornwall. Kevin still lives on his own in a flat in Alvaston still in Derby. He never remarried but he stayed friends with Julie often going to Cornwall on a visit.

Both his girls Claire and Kathryn are grown up now with families of their own .Julie had suffered with ill health for many a year. But I still stayed in touch with her via facebook we used to play games against each other with a lot of banter and had many a chat.

Julie had gone into hospital yet again and after having another operation she wasn't recovering has expected. Then came the call that nobody wants it was Kevin in tears over the phone saying that Julie had passed away with her loving family at her side. I was gutted just couldn't believe it. It was such a sad day that such a kind caring gentle person had gone a great loss to family and friends.

Kevin still goes to Cornwall to see the girls and family .although he suffers from ill health now. But he enjoys seeing the girls and the Cornish sea air must make him feel better.

So once again with a heavy heart I have to say to such a lovely brave lady Julie Scaife Rest In Peace.

Julie scaife 18-12-1956 - 6-2-2019

Michael

Michael was born 4th in line to what was now a growing family. I use the word family very loosely. Michael was truly the wild one. He definitely had the Scaife trate but had it bad. I can't really remember that much about us as kids. Just that he was always drunk barely able to stand sometimes. Wanting to fight anyone and everybody. Always in bother and always wearing a bandage on his hands, his face was the owner of the battle scars.

I've got to keep this short because I have no idea what happened to him or where he is at this moment in time. I just hope that he his happy, safe, and well.

Angela

Now we get to me. Born the first girl joining her brothers on the 10th November 1962 the much awaited baby girl. But when I arrived I was not welcomed by the father at all. From day one he never bonded with me and I always knew he disliked me enormously for whatever reason.

There were times I thought he actually hated me, strong words I know but that was how I felt all through my childhood. He was so cruel to me he would hit out at me for no reason, pull my hair, shout in my face, push me around.

His big thing was to send me down to the cellar to put money in the meter it was cold , dark, and wet down their but he found it funny to lock the door behind me shouting don't let the rats get ya.

You could hear him laughing while I scrambled to the top step crying and screaming for him to open the door. But he only opened the door when he felt like it.

So I will go has far as calling him a bully. Not the kind of father you could say you were proud of infact far from it. I wasn't the only one he would lock down there but I'll come to that later.

All he ever cared about was the booze, betting on the horses. That's where his money went , not on providing for his family. Not feeding his family, not buying clothes, or making the house into a nice home for the family. Hell no not a cat in hell chance.

Don't get me wrong he did work. He worked at Celanese for years in Derby based in Spondon . He walked there and back or though sometimes he did get the bus. He was a hard worker and that's about the only good thing I can say about him to be honeset.

Wendy

Not long after me the birth of another baby girl arrived named Wendy Caroline. Fathers little bundle of joy. Has she grew up she knew how to play the game . She was a very strong headed kid and she made sure that everyone knew she was there . She was a born

Show off she could do no wrong in the eyes of her father and she quickly knew it as well. So she milked it for all it was worth. She would sit beside him by the coal fire while he dryed her hair after her bath. Always allowed to have the bath first in a old tin bath that was kept outside on the wall of a old brick shed. When he had eaten and didn't finish it he would give any left overs to Wendy. He really did favour her. I wasn't the only one to see this. Again you will learn more later. If she wanted to get me into trouble with him she would start screaming and crying knowing full well he would come into the room shouting at me "

What the hell have you done to her?" When I said I didn't do anything i'd get a good hiding . While she lay on the sofa smiling. I really hadn't touched her but by the time he had finished with me all I really wanted to do was smash her in the face but I didn't dare.

Trevor.

On the 18th january 1965 another baby boy was added to the so called family Trevor Alan Scaife made his apperance. From what i remember he was a cute baby chubby face and a mass of black hair. Once again i don't remember much about what he was like has a child but i know we bonded we used to play out a lot together on the rubble of Wilmot Street and Sacheveral Street everything had been knocked down so that became our playground it was also used has a short cut to the local corner shop Savagers . Owned by Mrs s\Savage and her son Derek and daughter Jane, i think it is still there empty of course just left decaying away.

Trevor was the only one really that i got on with mainly because he was treated much the same as me he suffered at the hands of father .neither of us liked him . We were both scared of him.

Dawn.

Dawn Helen was the next baby girl to arrive born a diva, demanding and a proper drama queen. Blonde hair blue eyes looking quite angelic but she was far from it she turned into a two faced , dishonest , person will only do something if there was something in it for her, a user . Very good at manipulating people. But it didn't work on me .the less said about her really the better.

Martin.

And yes you guessed it another baby arrived. Another boy Martin John arrived on the 18 November 1967 the final one to have the miss fortune to be born into this so called family. He was a quiet kid really think he was just has troubled has the rest of us. We had so much to deal with has young kids. And to be honest has he grew up he to drifted away and to this day I don't know where he is or what his life turned out to be like . I do hope he his safe and well and above all happy.

Chapter 1

So where to begin? . At last no more babies. Why they had so many children when it was obvious they didn't want us is just a mistery . They couldn't afford so many and certainly showed no love. Infact they never used the love word to any of us or each other. That word was never used in the Scaife house hold.

I've spoken to Trevor about this and he agrees they never told us that they loved us.

Mother was a woman who liked a drink just has much as him, even though if you asked her about it she would deny ever being a drinker which makes me laugh to be honest. This is something else Trevor and I have spoken about so we can't both be wrong.

Mother was born Pauline Walker on march 13th 1937 which makes her 87 years old to date and do you know what …. She hasn't changed abit still stubborn still uncaring so hard and still doesn't give a damn. She's on parr with the man she was married to in a way they suited each other. To this day I will never inderstand her

Mother also had a violent streak in her. I remember one morning before school she was trying to put a school ribbon in my hair, my hair was long blonde and thick but for some reason she was getting mad with it or me not sure which but the next thing was a bash on the top of my head with the wooden hairbrush she had hit me so hard on top of my head I thought my head was split oh my God the pain was terrible I had a headache all day. The top of my head was so tender for weeks. All she could do was shout at me to stand still.

There was another time when she showed her vile temper. I'm not sure what I had done wrong but whatever it was resulted in her chasing me up the stairs with one of her white stiletto heeled shoes I thought she wouldn't catch me but she bloody well did and boy did I feel the wrath of that shoe. She was like a crazy woman.

I had bruises and a dent in the top of my leg for weeks, red and swollen and painful I couldn't touch it to bath it the pain just ran through me.

Mother showed that she could stand up to anybody including father. And she did just that on many occasion they used to fight like cat and dog neither of them came out the winner. I wondered then hasI do now why they were ever together. ??

I would very often walk to School crying either I had been shouted at or smacked again for some reason. There was a Traffic Warden who helped us cross the road on Bradshaw way. I remember her stopping me one morning and taking me to one side and asked if I was alright. But of course I wasn't but I never told her that I had just had a goodhiding from mother but I sensed she sort of knew .

Our grandparents Grandma and Grandad Walker used to live in the area of Allenton in Derby so when we wasn't at school mother used to walk us from our house in Leopold street , along Osmaston Road into the Allenton area of Derby to see them . I loved it when we went to see them. They had a lovely house so homely and cosey and such a beautiful garden it was full of flowers and it smelt lovely all the different smells from the flowers and plants. The garden was kept just like the house tidy and neat and smelled devine.

Now Grandma and Grandad never liked father and they made sure he knew it especially Grandma. From the first time she laid eyes on him she made it clear that she didn't like him and ever spoke to him not that she saw much of him. He never went to see them and to be honest he would have not been welcomed.

Has far as I'm concerned she had good reason not to like him he was a nasty cruel man and I think Grandma and Grandad could read him like a book. They knew only too well what he was like but when they tried to tell Pauline not to marry him she wouldn't listen. So she made her bed and that was that.

When mother took us to see Grandma and Grandad she would have two in a babies in the pram, one on a pram seat one under the pram itching a ride on the wire basket which was really meant for shopping but since there wasn't much shopping done it was used as a way to transport one the smaller kids. Then there would be a kid holding the handle of the pram one each side. The rest would just trail behind.

When we were ready for home Grandad used to give us a two and a half pence bit to buy sweets on the way home. When he gave me mine I used to look at it has though he had just given me the world it sure was a treat and a very welcomed one at that, the hug and kiss they gave when we were leaving felt good it was the only time we ever got such kindness. And boy could you buy a lot of sweets with it back in the day I had to spend it quick before it was taken away from me. We used to call in at a sweet shop on the way home along Osmaston Road.

We never had a family holiday; come to think of it we never had birthdays either. I remember being at school in the assembly when the head master asked me to stand up I was wondering what I had done wrong.

To my surprise the whole school started to sing Happy Birthday to me which is something they always did when it was someone's birthday. But the funny thing was I didn't even know it was my birthday. It was a surprise to me but I blagged it and smiled.

I used to like going to School it was nice to be away from everything and everyone for a short time. I was never very clever at School although I did enjoy English and Cookery.

3

The only thing was I did used to get bullied a lot at play time. I remember two girls inperticular that would corner me at break time push me from one to another kay was the leader with Debra being her partner in crime. They made fun out of me because they had a lot more than I did. I always felt scruffy compared to them. But it was still better than being at home. At least it was only at lunch times and break times and I could try to keep out of the way.

Another reason I used to like school was lunch time. I was so hungry by the time it reached 12 o'clock I could have eaten a horse. But no matter how hungry I was I tried to be at the end of the queue because that meant I would be one of the last in the dining room and still there when the dinner ladies shouted "does anyone want seconds?"

I was up there quicker than lightning. I loved the sponge cake with pink custard or the spotted dick with custard it was so warm and filling.

Before I knew it the bell was ringing for home time, I must have been the only kid who didn't like that last bell of the day. So I knew I had to drag myself back home if you could call it that. I would say more like a bloody mad house than anything else.

I would say that Tuesday was the best day of the week from what I can remember; you see Tuesday was family allowance day which meant mother had some money.

Which also meant hotpot and dumpling for tea if mother felt like cooking! But it was warm and filling, it was also rare for us to come home from school and be hit by the smell of cooking it truly was a rare treat.

Now Friday was a different day all together. Father would get paid and he would sometimes bring home our tea which consisted of apple, cheese and an onion cut up and shared out between us. I hear you ask what sort of tea is that.? Well we never questioned it we were all grateful for anything believe me.

Friday evening was the night father would send me to Nickies Fish Bar on Osmaston Road on the Spot to get fish and chips for him. He didn't even buy anything for mother, just himself the mean old bugger.

With the smell of the chips with salt and vinegar on them it just made me more hungry, it was too much to bare. Even though Nickie had given me a bag of scratching to eat and I made sure I eat the lot before reaching home.

Little did father know that on my way back carrying his fish and chips I would stop in a shop doorway, unwrap the package break of the end of the fish and help myself to a hand full of chips and boy did they taste good I could have quite easily have eaten the lot but instead I wrapped them back up and carried on my way home.

To this very day he never knew what I did. It was a risk and I would have paid the price for it had he found out but it was so worth it.

Again Wendy would get his left over's and she would smile at me but this time I'd smile back thinking to myself if only you knew, if only you knew.

This was the one time I felt like I had actually got one over her so I smiled to myself.

It was the same when Mrs. Savage from the corner shop saw me passing by just before closing time. She would call me in and give me a box of cream cakes that hadn't been sold. She'd say 'take these home and share them out'. I took them gladly and with a smile and a thank you I went on my way. But again I would stop in the same shop door way and eat at least two of them before going home.

Savagers was the shop mother would send me with a list of things like bread, milk , eggs, and five park drive cigarettes for father all on tick which meant she would pay for them at the end of the week.

Mrs. Savage was a kind caring woman her son and daughter used to help run the shop and they were all very kind to us. They always let us have things on tick they never said no unless the week before bill hadn't been paid.

I'm guessing Mrs. Savage isn't with us any longer and I'm not sure what happened to Derek and Jane. I know the shop is still standing empty and practically falling down now. It's such a shame that shop has been there for has long as I can remember.

We lived on Leopold street in Derby for some time. It wasn't far from Savagers.

The house was very big all the rooms were big although there was a box bedroom which I sometimes had has my bedroom.

The house consisted of a down stairs a large front room, hallway another room with a room connecting to it which had French doors that was the room our dog Peggie lived she was a black and white colley dog a friendly dog never any bother. I remember going into see her one morning only to find out she had given birth to a litter of puppies being only young myself I woundered where she got them from. They were all black and white so cute for some reason we kept one and named him bobby.

Then there was another room which I suppose would have been a dining room with the kitchen off that room.

None of the rooms had wall paper, carpet or any kind of decoration at all; it was the most coldest unwelcoming house ever. That was one of the reason none of us had friends round to play. I always felt ashamed if a friend knocked on the door asking if I was allowed out to play.

The only nice thing about the house was the coloured glass that was in the front door , well until Michael smashed it in one of his drunken rages, then it was just replaced by a large piece of cardboard which wasn't much use at all it let in the wind rain making it colder than ever.

Up stairs to the right was a large bedroom, bathroom and a separate toilet. Along the landing was a bedroom, then along the corridor were three more bedrooms and again no carpet or wallpaper.

There was a large stair case that had a long banister running at the side of the stairs to hold onto. We used to slide down it to entertain our self's. Well until Wendy had a go and fell off it onto the other side she hit the concrete floor with such a thud. She screamed and cried out, mother came running to see what was going on to find Wendy flat out on the floor and me just standing there not knowing what to do.

Guess who got the blame for it ….. Yeap me. Surprise surprise. Mother shouting at me telling me how stupid can you get?, are you bloody stupid? Why did you let her do it? What a stupid thing to do.

Wendy milked it of course laying on the sofa for days at a time with her blanket over her in front of the fire.

One morning I was getting ready for school doing my hair in front of the mirror which hung over the fire. Wendy was laying there laughing at me because I had to go to school and she didn't. I told her to shut up or I would hit her, but before I got the chance she was crying again with a added scream I looked at her in amazement mother yet again came in to see what was going on. Wendy laying there saying that I had smacked her in the face which I hadn't so mother turned on me hitting me in the face shouting how do you like. ? I never had a chance to deny it any way it wouldn't have made any difference.

So I took the smack in the face and with a red hand mark across the face it was another morning I went to school crying.

I was glad to leave my junior school. I moved to Homelands School which was in Littleover It seemed such a big school. I remember walking up the very long path way to the main entrance. The first day there was very daunting. I was dressed in a uniform which had been supplied by the

Council Well Fare. So at least I looked like everyone else. It was at Homelands School I met two very good friends Dawn and Grace they looked after me. I would spend so much time with Grace her mother a kind lady said we were joined at the hip, I went there for tea once after School I had never seen so much food the whole table was laid out with different foods, foods that I had never seen before let alone eaten. But oh my God it was good so tastey. For the first time I was so full I really couldn't fit any more food into my tummy if I tried.

I also spent time at Dawn's house again her mum used to feed me I remember the doorstep cheese sandwich she used to make me with a cold glass of milk oh boy crusty bread it was like being in heaven.

We are still friends to this day. Infact I went to Graces Wedding and she came to mine she's been a great friend to me over the years and we still keep in touch.

Being bullied at home wasn't enough I was bullied at School as well so the feeling of being unloved and unwanted was overwhelming I tried to run away a few times but I never had anywhere to run to apart from my brothers house. As I said David used to live on Douglas Street so I would run to his house without stopping only to cross the roads.

He would let me stay there for a night or two then he would send me home. When I was home no one asked me where I had been or if I was alright so I would just go up to my room. Then it was back to business has usual.

On Saturday s father would get up and get ready to go out. When mother asked where he was going he'd say" to the Old Market Hall to get something for dinner I'll be back in abit.''

The Market Hall was a great old building it was built in 1866 and its to this day still standing although it has had a makeover.

Its full of different stalls selling anything you could want from fresh fruit and veg to key cutting, getting your shoes reheeled to flowers infact you could but just about anything there.

Anyway father did go out but didn't return .So I was sent to find him. I was told to go to the Noah's Ark by mother. Mother knew just where to find him.

Sure enough when I reached the pub I put my head around the door and there he was sitting at the bar with a pint in one hand and a ciggie in the other.

I shouted him a few times before he turned round and shouted to me wait outside. So I waited and waited then eventually he came out wanting to know why the hell I was there coming to the pub making a scene , which I don't really think I did.

I told him that mother had sent me to find him to see if he had got anything for dinner yet. But of course he hadn't. I was told to follow him.

We crossed the road, made our way into the Market Hall where he brought potatoes, sausages, and a large tin of processed peas which I hated and still hate now. Mother used to make a gravy from the juice of the peas bloody horrid.

He gave the bag of shopping and told me to take it home. We crossed the road again, he went straight back in to the pub while I struggled to carry the shopping home.

We never saw him again that day , well not until the pub closed and he came staging home through the door. Straight into the wrath of mother and off they went again arguing, swearing at each other she would throw something at him, he would throw it back then we would hear him falling up the stairs swearing then he managed to get to bed.

At last it went quite again. And to be honest that was just the way things were in our house it was just the norm. We just got used to it. Living a bloody nightmare.

9

Before I leave this chapter I want to give a mention to someone who was very special to me.

At the time we lived on Leopold street and on the corner of Leopold Street right at the bottom on the opposite side to us was a massive house and there lived a elderly couple named Mr. and Mrs. Bagg.

They were a very kind caring couple. So kind to me. When they saw me saw me passing by or I would knock there door they always asked me in. The house was massive and in the hall way on the right hand side was a chair not just any chair but the most beautiful rocking chair the wood was so shiny. I loved it.

Mrs. Bagg always encouraged me to sit in it which to be honest I didn't need to be told twice. Mr. Bagg would bring me a glass of cold milk with some biscuits and we would sit and chat about what I had been doing at school.

I never left the house without them giving me something whether it is comics or a little doll. Not a Barbie or Cindy doll but something like it but I loved it just the same.

I don't know why they were so kind to me but I was and still am very grateful for that.

When we moved away I wrote to them every week keeping them updated on how I was doing and they wrote back. It was a lovely feeling when I received their letters.

I was saddened when I heard that Mr. Bagg had passed away and that Mrs. Bagg passed away a short time after.

I never forgot them and never will. For all their kindness they showed me I will be forever grateful.

R.I.P.. Mr. and Mrs. Bagg.

Chapter 2

It was the Derby City Council that moved us out of Leopold Street because the house had become too big for us now that the older ones had moved out into their own homes. We moved to Moncrieff Crescent in Chaddesden, by this time I was 16 years old and at the age where father couldn't treat me how he wanted to.

I had got myself a job at Debenhams in the Derby Town Centre where I worked for a year. So me having a job meant that I had money.

Father wasn't slow about coming for me when he knew it was payday. So now it was me he was waiting for. There he was like a bloody puppy waiting at the door for me to get home. But I wasn't go to give him the board money but I made of point giving it to mother each and every week.

Board money was for a bed and food, I had the bed but there was little food in the house same old story. Nothing had changed just a different house.

By this time I had a serious boyfriend and to be honest I spent most of my time with him. We even lived with his Grandma Alice who was old and not in the best of health, we helped her around the house, shopping but she got really ill so it was best if I moved back home. I spent the odd night at my boyfriend's parent's home in Littleover.

I managed to get a full time job at Birds in the Eagle Centre I actually loved working there.

Father used to come down and wait for me outside the shop but I just ignored him. Even at lunch time he was still there waiting for me or for my wages really. I ended up going out to him to tell him to go away has I hadn't been paid yet.

This was back in the day when you got paid weekly and your money was in a little brown packet.

I knew what he wanted the money for but I wasn't going to give it to him to go and piss up the wall. I had to work hard for my wage so I wasn't going to give it up to him.

I used to buy bread and ham, cream cake from Birds. After work I would get the bus home and pay mother my board money. I knew father wouldn't like it but hey ho!

Once she was paid I would go into my bedroom which I had made pretty and warm and cosey. I sat on the bed eating my bread, ham and then I enjoyed my cream cake washed down with a can of pop.

Then I would wait for my boyfriend to finish work at Samways on Ashbourne Road and he would come pick me up and we would go to his parents house in Littleover.

If it was my day off the next day I would sleep over and spend the day with him.

When I was 19 we got married and lived together in a small flat on Prince Charles Avenue in Mackworth. It was our place which was warm well decorated and a place we called home.

When I was nearly 21 we had our first baby a boy who we named Martin Stuart coming in at a healthy 8lb 8oz. But I don't remember actually giving birth. You see on the night I was in hospital I developed a terrible head ache which is all I do remember.

I had passed out. The next thing I knew it was Thursday afternoon with my then husband standing at the bottom of the bed.

He told me that my blood pressure had hit sky high and had to have a emergency caesarean. I very nearly died and so did our baby.

I was kept asleep and slowly they woke me up. It was then I realised I had given birth. But no baby cot. I got abit upset not seeing my baby at the side of me. So my husband asked for the baby to be brought up from the nursery so I could see him.

I was in the hospital for two weeks, it took time to recover but it turned out all good in the end.

Baby Martin was not a good sleeper, he cried all night long if I put him down but even holding him rocking him from side to side didn't always work.

He wasn't much better in the day either. He was quite a sickly baby always throwing his milk back up, when I was weening him he would throw that back has well.

But he was a clever little boy he was walking before he was a year old; the health visitor said he was advanced for his age. But has soon has he was old enough to do what he wanted to do he became such a happy little boy.

When he started school the teachers said he was above average all his school reports were outstanding and he continued to do very well at school. His grades were brilliant.

Then we went onto having our second baby. A girl Sarah Jayne weighing in at 8lb 7 ½ oz with a mass of black hair just like her daddy. She was just so beautiful. So different from her big brother. She hardly ever cried, only every two hours when she knew it was time for her feed. She to grew quickly into a beautiful toddler who knew what she wanted and how to get it. Sarah was a very independent toddler wanted to do everything herself even though she wasn't big enough.

Sarah was also a very bright clever little girl and has she grew it came shining through just how clever she was.

She has grown into a wonderful wife and mother of three beautiful children who are just like her in many ways. Sarah has never been the sort to take shit from anyone and I wish I was like that in my younger days.

When I was heavily pregnant with Sarah we moved from the flat into a three bedroom house on Woburn Place still in

Mackworth. Infact it turned out to be a stone throw away from where Wendy lived with her then husband. She had gone on to marry and have four children of her own.

It was quite funny really because we became good friends. Looking after each other's children, I went there for coffee and she would come to me. We went shopping together in actual fact we used to have some good times.

Our house on Woburn place was lovely it had three bedrooms, bathroom upstairs and down stairs had a good size front room and kitchen. It owned a large garden which would have been great for the kids when they got older. The house was decorated by my husband and his dad. It was so cosey everything I had always wanted.

But that wasn't to last. My father in law who was such a lovely man he would do anything for anyone, he really was the father anyone would have been proud of and to have has there father.

It was in January 1987 when we got a call from my mother in law saying that she had called an Ambulance has father had had a stroke. It was snowing outside and so cold. I remember my husband trying to get the car started and drove off has quick has he could.

Sadly Denis passed away after being in hospital for a short time. We couldn't believe it such a shock. He had always wanted a little girl after four sons. So when Sarah was born not only was she the second grandchild but the first granddaughter. His face lit up when he came to the hospital after she was born a little girl at last he said, he was so happy standing there holding her for the first time. I know for sure that if he had lived she would have been spoiled by him and very much loved has was Martin. I know that he loved her even if he got to spend such a short time with her but I am so pleased he knew he had finally got his little girl.

After he passed away mother in law found it really hard after all they had been married many years. She struggled with everything. so wasn't looking after herself at all. So after much consideration it was decided that we would move in with her.

Giving up our lovely new home. We moved in and to be honest it wasn't easy. Remember I had two young children to look after, while everyone else got on with their life's I was expected to look after her as well has the kids. I did the house work , cooking etc. It was ok at first but it wasn't long before it started to take its toll on me.

I had a husband that was griving for his dad , a mother in law griving for her husband two small kids that didn't understand what the hell was going on. Plus I also was griving I did miss him he was always good to me.

Soon I started feeling the stress of it all I had ear infections, couldn't sleep and our relationship was suffering. The arguments started and I just couldn't cope. I felt out of things and conversations when the family did come round it was alright for them they would visit at weekends not knowing anything that was going on in the week.

On one occasion Martin had picked up his Granddads watch toddling towards me with it he was trying to say Granddads watch he didn't understand what had happened it broke my heart he loved his Granddad. I picked him up and cuddled him he looked at me with his big eyes has to say what's up with you?

In the end it all became so over whelming I admit I wasn't coping at all.

One day while my husband was at work and mother in law was in town I got ready and took myself and the kids down to the local City Council I sat explained the situation and asked them for help.

When I told my husband that the Council were going to rehouse us he wasn't to happy. But he did come round to the idea. Looking back he must have felt like piggy in the middle. But we soon had the keys to our new house and moved in. This time it was on Carson Road Chaddesden Derby. Another three bedroom house so we had to start all over again. I admit it wasn't a good feeling leaving his mother on her own I felt guilty but I had to do it for my little family and my sanity.

We turned the house into a home carpets, decorating each room. Martin's room had a nice new blue carpet with blue wall paper with white clouds on it, his bed was pushed up against the wall giving him plenty of room to play with his many toys.

Sarah had the smaller room with new pink carpet her cot was placed under the window with all her soft toys displayed on shelfs that her daddy had put up.

The kids soon settled down into the new home has we all tried to get back to some sort of normality.

Mother in law seemed to be doing better, she had sold the bungalow and moved to StensonRroad in Littleover a big house on the main road. We would visit her at least once a week sometimes more.

Has she was doing so well she took driving lessons and passed her test first time. This meant she could get out and about and come to us whenever she wanted to.

My own mother used to come up on a Thursday at 12 o'clock and spend the day having her dinner and tea with us after watching Coronation Street my husband then gave her a lift home. By this time she and father had split and were divorced and not before time if you ask me. She now lived in a small three bedroomed house inLlittlover on her own , well until Dawn became a single mother to a baby boy. It was then that she stopped coming up to see us , but to be honest I wasn't to bothered she was hard work.

16

My mother in law then came to us on a Thursday or Friday night very often staying the night. While my husband was at work we would go out about in her car that she had brought for her self after she passed her test. The only thing was she kept having little bumps in it, reversing wasn't her thing.

She seemed to be doing so well even looked a lot better and seemed happy.

One night in December the 6th if I remember right she was at our house watching the tv after having a fish and chip dinner. Tonight she seemed different not her usual self . It had been snowing outside and was cold. It was around ten oclock at night when she decided to go home , I said just stay the night its horrible out there but she had made her mind up she wanted to go home.

When she went I always stood on the door step to wave her off but on this night she told me to go in has it was cold . So I did I went inside , went to the window and watched her drive off.

I turned to my husband and said bloody hell whats up with her tonight ? She was hard work today in a right mood.

Friday morning the 7th of December was just an ordinary day husband at work , i had taken Martin to the nursery and Sarah was playing in the front room with all her toys everywhere.

It must have been about 2.30 i was starting to get ready to go out and get Martin when there was a knock at the door when i opened it there stood two Police Officers asked if i was Angela and could they come in.

Once they were in the front room one Officer made a b line for Sarah and started paying her attention . The other Officer started asking me questions about my mother in law. When was the last time you saw her? What time did she leave here? Had you heard from her when she left here? I didn't understand why they were asking.

When i asked what was going on the reply was she been in a accident my response was oh God what has she hit now? She was always hitting a post or something. I asked if she was alright the Officer informed me that she was in the D.R.I. (Derby Royal Infirmary). So i asked how bad is she hurt ? Tell me what ward so i can go down to see her.

But i wasn't expecting what he said next.

It turned out that a dog walker had found her still in the car only there was a hose pipe connected to the exhaust pipe , engine still running and the windows were all black from the fumes. There was a bottle of sherry and a box of paracetamol at the side of her. He had smashed the window to get the door opened and pulled her out but it was to late she was gone.

I couldn't believe what i was hearing , my legs went to jelly and i was shaking . I phoned my husband telling him he needed to come home straight away. Then i phoned the rest of the brothers telling them they needed to come as soon as possble. We were all in a massive state of shock.

Once everyone was gathered at our house i was taken to the D.R.I. Mortuary to identify her body. She was lying on a bed with a white sheet covering her up to her neck, her face was pale but her hair and makeup still looked like it always did. She was still wearing the same clothes from the night before when she had left our house.

I just stared at her for what seemed ages then i heard a voice from behind me saying can you just say yes or no. I muttered yes. I was taken out the room and given a glass of water before the Officer took me home.

When i got home i walked into the front room my husband and his brothers with their wifes looked at me i looked back and said its her.

I attended the Inquest with my brother in law and his wife we got to hear everything and meet the man that found her. He was quite a big well built man and after giving his

Evidence he came over to us and expressed how very sorry he was. We thanked him for trying shook his hand and parted waves.

I couldn't help but feel so very sorry for him , he was in tears and so were we. I just hope he could put it out of his mind over time bless him , it must have been a shock for him.

So now this was something else we all had to try to overcome. Christmas that year wasn't the same but we did our best for the sake of martin and sarah. There were three other grandchildren by this point but thankfully all to young to understand what was going on.

My own mother was no where to be seen by this time and I hadn't seen father for years not that I missed him , if ever he had turned up he would have had the door slammed in his face.

He never really got to meet Martin or Sarah . I think the first time he did see them was when i went to see Wendy she had four children of her own by now so they would all play together. He turned up and actually lived there with his blue eyed girl not sure why or how he ended up there but he did. On this day i was there Sarah was toddlering past him when he smacked her bottom she started crying i picked her up and told him if he ever put a hand on her again id fucking kill him and at that i got the kids together and went home. If i had known he was going to be there i would never have gone. After that i didnt cross his path again until some years later.

Chapter 3

So it was hard trying to get over what had happened , life had to go on after all we had young chidren to think of.

But our marriage was slowly going down the pan for a lot of reasons .

We decided to buy our own house on Valley Road in Chaddesden , it was a lovely three bedroom house . We moved in after a few months later.

I suppose we were happy there for a short time , it must have been about a year when things were still not right so i thought long and hard about the next decision . Finally i came to the conclusion that i was going to ask him to leave. Which i did. I just couldn't do it any more.

He wasn't happy with what i had to say and didn't want to go. Said he didn't want to leave . But i insisted it was for the best. So while he was at wotk i packed his suit case making sure he had everything he would need. All clean clothes, toiletries etc. . It was all ready for when he got home from work. He was still insisting that he didn't want to leave , but i knew it was for the best .

Has timed passed we got used to it he had found somewhere to live and soon found someone else and is still with her to this day.

On the other hand i had starting going out at the weekends with my friends while the kids were at there dads. I was having a good time i suppose , i was catching up with myself after spending years of being a wife and a mother. Now the kids were getting older i felt i could have abit of me time.

The kids were growing up fast now but they also started to play me up has kids do . I was the baddie i suppose i was the one who said   the word "no" . I was the one who tried to keep them going to school, i was the one who clamped down on there behaviour when they miss behaved. They obviously didn't like this . But i tried to be a good mum to them both doing what i thought was the right thing. I had to be hard on them at times , i was the Mum and Dad at home . It wasn't easy but i loved them i just wanted the best for them.

Sarah was being bullied at School but dispite me going up to the School seeing the Headmistress and making a fuss it didn't seem to make any difference. She hated School it was that bad she wouldn't even go to the school prom when the time came.

Has much as i wanted her to go she was determind she wasn't going , so that was that.

Such a shame really because she was a clever girl her school reports were good her grades were good and dispite the bulling her attendance was good although i later found out she had been bunking off going to her cousins flat which wasn't that far from our house. Seemed she had spent her breaktimes and dinner times there as well.its funny what you find out about your own kids once they have left School it proves that with all the will in the world you never truly know has much has you think you do! Martin was also doing his own thing . He loved to play football he played for Derby Boys and Chesapeake Football Club for a few years. He won Thropies , Man of the Match . Many a Sunday morning was spent watching him play football in all sorts of weather. But that also was to come to a end he had quite a few injuries in the time he played from a broken nose , to breaking his leg it was that injury that finished his playing the game he loved.

He went in for a tackle but ended up with a broken leg , he ended up having a operation on his leg and having it pinned he was out of action for months. His leg was in a brace . So that was that he was advised by the hospital not to play football . He still loves to have a kick about but not on the level he used to.

He had a good group of friends so he spent a lot of time with them. Doing what young lads do. Having a laugh , playing pool etc even going to pub when he was old enough of course.

They have both grown now with families of there own and i am so very proud of them both. I must have done something right because they turned out to be kind and caring people . So like i said im proud of them. They had both been through a lot during there young lifes but managed to over come it .

Chapter 4

I was still going out on the weekends with the girls i was meeting different men but none of them seemed to last. I thought it was me , what was wrong with me?

I decided just to have fun go with the flow and enjoy myself .then when i wasn't expecting it i meet someone . He was a doorman he started to pay me attention Mr Charmer .

I was quite struck on him at first dispite being warned to stay away from him, hes trouble, he likes the ladies, hes a lier he will end up hurting you hes a player but i didn't listen for some reason and that was a massive mistake , all the above and more actually came to path.

None of my family liked him , Martin and Sarah definitely didn't like him. My friends tolerated him for my sake. But still i carried on seeing him. He caused me more heart ache than anyone deserved.

After a while we called it a day. But he couldn't leave me alone . I started going out with the girls avoiding going to where he worked the doors. I would come home to so many missed calls from him.

Because i had been drinking i got brave so i phoned him to ask why he had been phoning me. He said he wanted to get back with me it was a mistake to finish it with me. The next thing i knew he was on the door step. And that was that he had charmed his way back in.

Just after that and without me knowing he had taken Martin and Sarah to one side to tell them he was going to ask me to marry him , he wanted to know their thoughts .Martin made his feeling clear and said no he didn't want me to marry him and Sarah's response was much the same.

But he asked me anyway. I must admit i went into shock because i wasn't expecting it. Like a fool i said yes. Before i knew it he had given up his house in Oakwood Derby and was moving in with us. It was during this time i got a phone call from Trevor saying that father was ill and didn't have long to live. Since i hadnt seen him for years i didn't feel anything or say anything. He asked me to come to the hospital to see him. I was surprised by that Trevor was obviously more forgiving than me. I didn't go. Then another phone call to say he had died and did i want to see him before they removed him from the room he was in? I yet again I said no . But Trevor was persistant so i went. Ive never seen such performances bloody crying and dying swan acts anybody would have thought he was the father of the year. I went into the room to see him all laid out and i felt nothing , nothing at all. I turned away walked out and that was it he was gone at the age of 70 .The funeral which i went to with Trevor and his wife was mind blowing the sight of all the brothers and even mother sitting there crying i sat and looked and asked my self why???????? We didn't attened the wake it was more than i could cope with all the acting which if on TV would have won them an Oscar. I never really saw any of them after that , mother had distanced herself not just from me but most of her children, apart from her beloved Dawn and her son. You would think she hadnt got any other children and grandchildren it was Dawn this , Dawn that the only pictures she had on her wall was Dawn and her son . I had given her many a school photo of Martin and Sarah but when i asked where they were the answer was oh ive put them somewhere! The next time we got to see each other was when our brother Stuart passed away that was in2017 . So life returned to him making himself at home .

Now that was just the beginning of a long path of heart ache and misery. If there is one thing in this life that i regret is ever setting eyes on him . And that's the truth.

We had our hen/ stag night on the same night but i made sure we went to different places on that night. All went well , had a good time with the girls . Then i arrived home first , a few minutes later he returned home absolutely hammered he couldn't stand up. Thankfully his best man was with him and tried to sort him out. But he was in a mood for some reason and started going wild he hit out at me and slapped me so hard in the face he nearly knocked me over.

His best man had got him on the floor , then there was a knock on the front door it was the Police someone had called them . They asked if i was ok and did they want us to take him, his best man assured them he was ok now and was going to sleep it off. So they went.

To this day he never knew who called the Police that night it really got to him not knowing , but i know who it was but never told him.

The next morning was horrible. The kids were in a state , they had been so scared the night before , Sarah had gone into Martins bedroom and they blocked the bedroom door so he couldn't get in.

But for some unknown reason i went stayed with him . What the hell was i thinking ? What was wrong with me ? Why did i let him talk me around?

I always knew it wasn't going to end well.

We got married in 1999. Even on the day i had my doubts , woundering if i should go through with it but i remember thinking ive got to do it everything is booked and paid for the car was on the way.

So very foolishly i went ahead with it. Even at the reception he disappeared for ages people were asking me where is he? I couldn't answer them because i didn't know.

He had two young sons who came to the wedding but i don't think they were very impressed with him. And i didn't blame them he definitely wouldn't win any father of the year.

Not long after the wedding my heart ache began. Martin moved out and went to live with his dad. He just couldn't live with him they didn't get on and Martin really didn't like him.

Sarah had row after row with him. I have to admire her has she always stood up to him telling him how it was. She didn't mince her words when they were arguing she was quite a fire ball she didn't take any shit from him.

Has soon has she was old enough she moved in with her boyfriend and had a baby boy. I used to go and see them i loved my first grandson from the day Sarah said she was pregnant. She made a brilliant mum.

But Sarah leaving meant that i was now on my own with him. I felt guilty my two children had been driven out of there own home by him and i didn't stop it.

I was grateful for the full time job i had at the Co-op Department Store in Derby. It turned out to be my sanctuary, my chance to get away from him for as long has i could.

I did any over time i could . I remember working nine days in a row just to keep away from him. I didn't mind working weekends . I loved it there i made some great friends. He worked shifts so by the time i got home he was at work so this worked well for me. It meant i could go days without seeing him he would get home from work just has i was going to work.

But this didn't stop him getting to me . He would phone up work giving me shit down the phone. I told him not to ring me at work upsetting me. In the end i asked switchboard not to put his calls through. But his next move was he started coming into the store. It just seemed there was no getting away from him. Being at work on the shop floor i had to pretend everything was good. But it certaintly wasn't.

Many a time i would keep asking myself the same questions why did i marry him? Why have i let him treat me like this? Why did i let him push my children away?

In my mind i was going crazy i believed everything he said but i don't know why i did.

He wasn't anything like the picture he had painted of himself in fact he was quite the opposite and more.

He even pushed me into Remortgaging my house that was part of my divorce from the kids dad. He promised to make the payments which i later found out he hadnt , yet another promise he had broken . Now the house was going to be repossessed if i couldn't sell it before a certain date. I was going out of my mind with worry and stress.

Our Marrage was sinking faster than the Titanic i felt like i was drowning. He liked his whisky but the whisky didn't like him it made him violent. He thought he could handle his drink but he only had to sniff it and he was pissed.

There was a occasion when he had been drinking i had to phone his sister for help as he had lost the plot , went mad , he had hit me once again. By the time his Sister had arrived he had fallen asleep on the sofa and that's where i left him for the rest of the night. His Sister not really saying a lot !

For years i had suffered from chronic back pain it got so bad i had to have a year off work having all different kinds of treatment which didn't work. The disc at the bottom of my spine was protruding out , not enough for them to operate has it could be dangerous .so for years this has limited me from doing a lot of things. However this did not bother him it meant that he could do his thing without me. I stayed at home most of the time while he was on nights out with his brother or the one friend he had.

Well i managed to sell the house before the dead line. But it fell through so it went back onto the market. It soon sold again and this time went through which meant i had to start packing and finding somewhere else to live.

The agents that sold the house helped with finding somewhere for us to move to, even though he would ring them up shouting at the staff. I got a call one day from the Manager at the Estate Agents saying he had been on the phone shouting at one of the ladies there and she was in tears. I couldn't believe it there was no reason for him to to act like this after all it was his fault we were in this position in the first place.

All i could do was apologise to her , but she said it wasn't for me to apologise i hadnt done anything wrong but said she appreciated it. Also saying that they were going to refuse any more dealings with him . They were only prepared to deal with me in future.

Eventually they found us a ground floor flat on Lauvain Road off Burton Road in Derby.I t was a two bedroom , open plan which suited me just fine.

By this time i had had to give up work due to ill health and boy did i miss going to work seeing the girls who made my day worth while. Id get surprised visits from Sarah and my little grandson which would cheer up. But now i am at home all day everyday.it was ok has Sarah was coming to see me now on a daily bases . She had had another two sons by now so they kept us busy.

Martin would only come over to see me when he knew that he wasn't home and would go before he came home.

Our marriage was going down the pan quite quickly, we spent more time not talking . I was actually hating him more and more everyday. Even when he was a sleep id look at him and want to hit him in the face for everything he had done and said to me that day.

Considering when he had had a heart attack , had his hip replacement, and was diagnosed with diabetes i was there for him every minute of the day and night. I washed him, shaved him, changed his clothes for him he always had a clean tidy house. His clothes were always washed and ironed and yet he treated me like a dog.

He would continue to make fun of me in front of people, calling me fat and ugly, saying nobody would want me and i should be grateful i had him. Did i know just how many women would like to be in my place.?

His ego was massive . He loved himself more than anything or anyone. He would flirt with different women in front of me, making me look stupid in front of my friends, calling me names.

I saw how he behaved when i was there so it made me think how he behaved when i wasn't there. I remember one time he had gone out with his one friend into town for a night out. It was 12oclock at night when the house phone rang. It was his mate asking me if he was home has he couldn't find him he lost him in one of the pubs. He looked but couldn't find him anywhere. Well of course he wasn't home so where was he??? My mind was going into overdrive. I lay there wide awake waiting for him to show up.

It was turned 3.15 am when i heard the key go in the door. I pretended to be asleep. He went straight into the bathroom, after a while he came into the bedroom he smelt like he had been in a brothel all night. He undressed and slipped into bed.

I was up well before him the next day. So when he did finally get up i asked if he had had a good night, yeah he says wasn't to bad. So then i asked what time did you get in ? I never heard you come in (which i had) . It was about half past one he said which I knew was a lie which made me think he had something to hide.

So then i told him that his mate had rang at 12 o clock looking for him has he couldn't find you so where was you? He went mad whats with all the questions? Needless to say we had a row about it but to be honest i never found out the truth and i wasn't that bothered. I was well passed the stage of caring.

We didn't talk for quite a while , one of those days he stood up walking past me without warning he slapped me at the back of the head it knocked me for six. I looked at him and said that's going to be the last time you will ever do that . He burst out laughing at me saying what the hell do you think your going to do? Come on tell me what you going to do?

Again i looked up at him and told him that by the end of the week i was gone i was leaving him. Once again he laughed at me and where the hell will you go nobody wants you around. You are not going anywhere.

I spoke to Sarah and told her i wanted to leave. She was more than happy to help me . She spoke to her husband and started making plans for me to move in with them. This is something i will be forever grateful. By midweek he was still mocking me thinking i wasn't leaving but little did he know.

Two of the girls had come round to see me we were having a drink outside when he came out to us mocking me again saying have you heard shes supposed to be leaving me , but if she lost weight id be all over her. I looked at the girls and they were shaking their heads my response was hell your never going to touch me ever again. He turned and walked back inside the girls were disgusted with him. I was used to it by now. But it still hurt. I tried hard not to cry. I knew this was going to be the last time he would humiliate me.

Finally Friday had arrived i was excited but nervous because he was home when Sarah turned up to fetch me, she had emptied her car so we could get has many of my things in as we could. He stopped us from taking some things but it didn't matter. I just wanted out of there. Just before we were leaving he stopped me saying don't you want to take the Wedding album with you ? I asked why the hell would i want that? He said so you can look back and see what you've lost. Now it was my turn to laugh saying why don't you keep it so you can look back and see what a good thing you lost. I just got to door and the cheeky sod said hold on will you cook me some dinner before you go ? Hence i walked out gobbed smacked at what he just said.

Has Sarah drove away i smiled knowing that gone were the days when he could treat me like crap and talk to me in such a disrespectful way no more being bullied , no more slaps.

Chapter 5

So Sarah and her husband helped me to get settled into their home. It was great to be there , the feeling of being with them and the boys made me feel safe. The boys were great to be with they really took my mind off things and made me laugh so much they were happy kids made you smile even if you didn't feel like it. Just what the doctor ordered.

We did have some really fun days with the boys. Mind you we had some good nights as well. Girlie nights in at Sarahs were the thing . Great music , food, friends and of course being with Sarah was just brilliant.

I felt free at last it was a wired feeling really. Not having to worry about his moods . I really was free of him.

I had my own room has Sam had given up his room for me. He had moved his things into his brothers bed room , it was quite a big room just has well really . His two younger brothers had a bunk bed so there was room for his bed and all his toys, desk etc.

There are good boys and were growing quickly developing their own personalities , so funny . They made a fuss of me and it felt lovely the feeling of being wanted was over whelming i loved them all so much. I have to admit i lapped it up , every single cuddle , every single kiss they gave me . Being there when they went to bed and there when they got up in the morning , being there when they went to school or nursery and when they came home.

What good times they were. The memories i will always treasure and be for ever grateful to Sarah and her husband Guy for taking me in and looking after me in my hour of need .

When Martin heard that i had left him and moved in with Sarah he came to see me . The first thing he said was are you ok? Followed by about bloody time !

When i told the girls that i had finally left him they were happy for me and thought it was the best thing i could have done. We arranged a night out and Sarah managed to come as well .It was the best night ever.

When i started talking to the girls i was surprised just how happy for me they were one said to me that she had once overheard him being disrespectful to me and from then on she never liked him , she said if her husband had spoken to her that way he would be gone she wouldn't put up with it.

Everyone was saying how much better i looked and how much happier i seemed. I sure was feeling happier . Having the reassurance from everybody boosted my confidence as well made me feel like my old self again.

I don't know what came over me i felt like a puppy being let off his lead for the first time. Loving life once again. Doing what i wanted when i wanted to do it.

I lost weight but continued to loose weight but this soon became a concern to Sarah. She had reminded me that i hadn't eaten for days , why i don't know because she or her husband Guy cooked everyday but i just didn't feel hungry .

I tried to eat but after a few mouth full i was stuffed i just couldn't finish a meal. Looking back now i think it must have been a reaction to everything i had been through .

A few years before this i had to have a Operation on my mouth due to the Doctor finding mouth Cancer. I couldn't really eat much at the time but went onto to make a full recover. So with that and everything else i think the stress just took its toll on me. But i got through it with the help once again from Sarah.

I can honestly say i wouldn't have done so well if it wasn't for the care and support of Sarah and her wounderful husband Guy and of course the boys.

Chapter 6

After living at Sarah' s for quite a long time i thought it was time for me to get my own place now, it was time to let Sarah and her family get back to their normal family life . Let them spend time together they had baby sat me for long enough . It was time for me to move on.

Sarah came with me to the Derby City Council to see if they could help me. There were a lot of forms to fill in and a lot of questions to be answered, but it was worth it has i didn't have long to wait before they offered me a flat.

Sarah once again came with me to view it and i signed the papers there and then.

That week-end i was out with the girls again feeling so happy and free. I must have looked like a mad woman smiling all the time . Nothing was going to upset me now.

It was that night that i was in a bar called the Tiger Bar i had my drink and was dancing on the dance floor . It was then that i had noticed a man standing agaisnt the wall with a beer in his hand . Me being me I danced my way over to him and he smiled has i tried to pull him onto the dance floor with me, but he wasn't having any of it he shook his head no.

The girls were shouting Angie step away from the man. I was laughing so much and carried on dancing.

Funny thing was i noticed that there was something about him he had a good aura.. I continued to get him on the dance floor but he was stubborn he was having none of it but at least he was still smiling .

I wasn't deterred by this in fact it was as if he had thrown down the gaunlet and i was more than happy to take it.

Has the night went on i kept bumping into him in different pubs , he always throw that smile of his at me , i was feeling brave at this point so i made my way over to him. We started chatting and eventually with a bit of persuasion from me he added me on face book.

I thought about him for the rest of the night and woundered if he would contact me. But i need not have worried by the time i got home there was several messages from him. We chatted for a while and he was making me laugh. Then we made a date to meet up which we did . Then another date and another. It was brilliant we seemed to talk a lot and soon found out we had more in common that we thought.

By this time i was moving into my flat i didn't have a lot my coffee table was a box covered over with a cloth and a small lamp placed on top. There were two camping chairs to sit on, no curtains. It already had a cooker, fridge freezer and a washer. Sarah got me a microwave off a free sight which was like new.

Friend's rallied round getting me a toaster, kettle, bedding it was looking quite cosy. The bed was what i brought from my old place so i only needed a robe and bedside tables which another friend was giving away .It was coming together slowly although there was no carpets down. But it didn't matter. It was warm , clean and cosy.

Michael came round to the flat on on friday night and didn't go home till the Sunday evening . We seemed to be spending more time together . It felt like i had always known him we were so comfortable in each others company. We could talk for England .

We were talking one night and he told me that was married with four girls but was going through a divorce his soon to be ex wife had broken his trust and his heart.

I told him about my situation and he could relate to it. We had both been through the mill although it wasn't our fault , but in away i was glad i had gone through it other wise i wouldn't have meet Michael.

I know i said i wasn't ever going to have anything to do men again but there was just something about him that kept drawing me to him. I knew he was handsome and the way he carried himself was so attractive , he is quite a tall man with his black curly hair tied back , big brown eyes and those lips are so kissable.

The more we saw each other the more we got on and the more my feelings were growing for him. He was special , he was different it was that aura again it was strong. I tried not to fall for him has i thought it was to soon but i just couldn't help it. We had both said we wasn't going to use the love word but i knew i loved him and it wasn't long before we did use the love word . And boy it felt good.

Christamas was approaching and we were making plans to spend it together. Sarah had meet Michael a few times and seemed to like him , they got on straight away. Sarah and her friend had been round to the flat for drinks and food it was a good night lovely to spend time altogether.

Sarah had invited Michael and myself over to theres during the Christmas Period and it was a great night, everyone seemed to like Michael straight away. Sam took to him he showed Michael his Michael Jackson dance to I'm bad it was brilliant. Jake was the quiter one out of the boys and quite shy but even he took to Micheal , lucas wasn't very old but he followed Michael around and sat either with him or on him . The boys must have also picked up on his good aura.

After the Christmas period was done Michael had gone home after spending nearly two weeks at mine , once he had gone i felt lonely i was missing him so much i couldn't wait until he was back again.

Michael had asked me to go on hoilday with him, i thought about and decided to go i thought it would do me good , time to relax and unwound.

We went to Italy somewhere i had always wanted to go and it was has beautiful has i thought it would be , it was like a dream . We had a beautiful room with a balcony looking over the lovely views. The food and drink was plentiful , day trips , boat trips it was like a different world.

We walked , talked, laughed messed around on the beach it was such a wounderful time but the time to go home came only to quickly.

Italy will always be a special to me , great memories etched in my mind.

Chapter 7

When we got home we started talking about moving in together but the flat was a little too small for us both.

So because of me having a mad ex and Michael had a ex wife who was just has mad and had found out Michael was seeing someone else now so we thought it would be better if we moved away from Derby.

His ex had already started sending me messages on face book which were quite nasty. I ignored her and blocked her.

I had meet his daughters a few times by this point and they seemed nice we got on quite well. In the mean time my ex had found out where i lived and kept driving past he couldn't see me but i could see him in the car from my window.

Michael and i knew that if our relationship was going to stand a chance of working it would be better to move somewhere else where no one knew us and start a fresh.

We gave it a lot of thought has we also knew that this news would upset Sarah and the boys. I knew my friends wouldn't be to happy with me either which they weren't some more than others.

It wasn't that we wanted to upset anyone it just felt like the right thing to do. There were some that were happy for us and wished us well.

Martin wasn't fussed either way he was so busy with work and had brought his own house with his girlfriend so i knew he was happy and settled .

Sarah was gutted and very upset with me. I understand why though. After all we spent a lot of time together, we did most things together and she had looked out for me many a time. I also knew i would miss her so much and the boys .

Michael and i started to look for places to rent. We had a friend that lived in Cannock Staffordshire . We used to visit them at week-ends. It was those same friends that saw a bungalow on the market to rent in Hednesford not far from Cannock.

We quickly made arragements to go and view it , has soon has we pulled up in the car we both knew this was the one we loved it at first sight.

It wasn't long before the papers were signed , deposit paid and a moving date was set.

It was all very exciting for us both. I soon started packing my things and Michael began packing his room that he rented from a friend. I don't think she was very happy to be losing him but she got used to it.

Everything was ready to go. The night before we moved we stayed at my flat we had a takeaway and a beer and slept on the mattress on the floor. The next morning we went over the road to a small café for breakfast while we waited for the removal van to arrive.

Michael had already packed the car with the smaller things .At last the removal van arrived it didn't take long to load it up and before we knew it we were on our way.

Sarah didn't come to wave us off it was to much for her bless her.I had tears in my eyes as we drove away it was a mixture of emotions .

Finally we arrived at our new home , our first home together . By the late afternoon we had unpacked every thing , the bed was made everything had a place and it already felt like home. All the empty boxes had been flattened and put outside.

We sat down quite late that night had our first takeaway meal on the first night in our first home it was just magical. We had a drink to our new home, new memories and to a happy future.

We soon settled into our home, it felt like we had always lived there it sure was meant to be. We loved it.

But after the first week it was time for Michael to go back to work. That meant he was going to have to drive to Derby everyday which also meant i was going to be on my own for the first time since we moved in. I didn't really know anyone and i didn't really know my way around apart from the few shops that we had found together.

It was a long day for me but even a longer day for Michael has he had to drive to Derby which was an hours drive do a twelve hour shift then another hours drive home.

But as time went by i got used to it and started walking into the town and going around the shops . It was on one of my walks to the shops that i saw a neighbour out in her front garden i said hello and we got chatting and that was the beginning of a good friendship. Her name is Hazel and her husband Charlie. I asked her round for coffee and before long we were always at each others house having coffee and a chat which was company for me. We went into town shopping together and soon got to know each other, we had some laughs.

Our other friends Ric and linda who already lived in Cannock used to go to a club on a Saturday night they had asked us to go with them one Saturday which we did. It wasn't long before we asked Charlie and Hazel to come with us . We had some good nights we loved the music and the beer wasn't to bad either.

We started to make some friends there but there were some who didn't take to us purely because they are racist and didn't like Michael in the club. They didn't try to hide the fact either there were comments said which we were meant to hear but we chose to ignore them. This went on week after week.

One week Michael was tired so he decided we would go to the club but he wasn't going to drink so he drove. Now

41

one rule Michael has and as always kept to is no drink driving he had always stuck to that. He had to much to loose and he knew it was wrong.

That night when we got home i had just poured a rum and coke and took one sip when there was a knock on the door, now bare in mind it was 12 o'clock at night so when i opened the door to see two Police Officers standing there you can imagine what was going through my mind. The last time i opened the door to find two Police Officers standing there they had come to inform me my mother in law had been found in her car.

I did notice however that one of the Officers was touching the car on the bonnet which i thought was strange. He asked if i owned the car i said no its my partners and with that Michael came to the door.

They asked if they could come in as they had received a report that the driver of this car had been drink driving and was driving dangerously.

They came in and we explained that yes we had been to the club but Michael had not been drinking , he had only just had a sip of rum and coke when we got in. They were at our house for over an hour asking questions and did a test where Michael at to blow into a tube and await the results and of course it came back negative.

I explained this wasn't the first time things like this had happened with someone from the club, i told them it was a racist thing . We were offered the chance to report it but we decided not to after all what would be the point ?

After they apologized they left . By this time it was gone 1am so we went to bed but neither of us slept very well that night.

We had some friends that would come over from Derby at the week ends and often took them up to the club in a taxi . It was on one of those Saturday nights that it all kicked off. I had been in the ladies toilet when i over heard two women on about Michael calling him a dirty darkie i was fuming they had asked me if i was with the dark chap i said Michael , they repeated the darkie i repeated Michael ! They didn't like that so i turned and left them to it.

When i got back to where we were sitting there was a member of the club committee asking Michael if he had been sick in the men toilet he repeatedly said no he hadn't but she was not letting up. She insisted it was him.

I was getting stressed and felt horirble for Michael he's a big chap but so gentle hates confrontation of any kind. He sat there but i could see how upset he was. I felt so sorry for him , theres's nothing worse being accused of something that you know you didn't do. I had to go outside to calm down, that was when i overheard a group of people talking about Michael. I heard one say " that dirty darkie has been sick in the men toilet." At that i let them see me and made it clear that i had heard them. That stopped them in their tracks. I went onto say " don't stop chatting on my account carry on what was you saying? It went quite for a minute but then they surrounded me shouting in my face, arms going everywhere trying to intimidate me but little did they know this was not new to me i had been used to this sort of thing all my life so i gave has good has i got.

Before i knew what was happening Michael, and the friends we had took with us were outside along with me, they had been asked to leave . So we did . But i didn't leave it there i wrote letters of complaint to the Head of the Committee the only reply i got was a letter pushed through my door a few weeks later telling me (not asking me) to attend the club on a Sunday to answer the chargers for example swearing ! I wrote back telling them i had no intention of being there . I returned the membership cards telling them that we did not want to be Memebers of a racist club. They should be a shamed of them selfs. And that was that.

It didn't take us long to find somewhere else to spend our Saturday nights. We would go into the town centre where we found a few nice bars which would soon become our regular place to go.

It was a few weeks later that we heard from a friend that someone had been sick in the men toilet at the club. I couldn't help it i laughed out loud. A friend had told the Committee that he was the one who had been sick previously and they were wrong to blame Michael and the way they had treated him was out of order and that she didn't want to be associated with the club any longer.

Chapter 8

We had settled quite nicely into our new home. Everything was going great . Michael had worked his magic on the garden and it was looking beautiful. Flowers had been planted, the grass had been cut and shaped . All the neighbours were saying how lovely it looked .

We had a lovely shed out in the back garden that we painted and made into a beach hut. We would sit in it at night with a glass of wine and enjoyed it.

It was on one of those lovely sunny days i was sitting in the back garden with a coffee, Michael had gone to work.

The phone rang it was my Auntie Linda i was quite surprised to hear from her pity it was she who broke the news to me. Asking me have you heard about Stuart? (my second eldest brother) i said no why whats up? She continued to tell me that he had passed away . I couldn't believe what she had just said. I went into shock.

The first thing i did was phone Michael to tell him. I was in tears i didn't understand what the hell i had just been told. Michael said its ok I'm on my way home.

I sat down wandering why mother had not phoned to tell me, what the hell is wrong with her?

I picked up the phone and rang her , she answered the phone more or less straight away. I said what the hell happened ? Why didn't you ring me? When did it happen ? Her response was well i knew you would find out sooner or later. I just said im sorry for your loss ill ring you later, but i never did.

I just couldn't speak to her i knew she had just lost her son and it must have been a shock to her as well but i cant get over the fact she didn't think about phoning me to tell me that my own brother had passed away.

Michael was back home before i knew it bless him. He just put his arms around me held me tight and let me cry. Then he made coffee while we sat and i told him what little i knew.

After that i phoned Stuart's wife Lesley . We were both crying has she tried to tell me that they were on a cruise when Stuart said he didn't feel well she managed to get him to the cabin and called the doctor but he had collapsed with a heart attack and died.

What a shock for Lesley, alone now on a big ship i can only imagine how she must have felt. When she arrived home all alone she was tasked with trying to get Stuart home which wasn't an easy task, but after some weeks he finally arrived home.

Then Lesley had made arrangements for the funeral. What a day that was Lesley had done him so very proud and to see Stuarts daughter Stacey help carry her dad into the chapel was so over whelming. Stacey also did her dad proud .

There were so many people that had attended his Service , people were having to stand at the back.

Mother was there of course with her daughter Dawn and her son. The only ones that ever mattered to her. Sitting stoned faced .

Trevor and Lisa sat one side of me while i held onto Michael not wanting to let him go. Wendy was there with her husband and family she sat along side me .

It was a beautiful service but then came the last post played by ex service men and that did it for me the tears came.

At the wake i sat with Michael one side and Trevor and Lisa the other side of me . Then there was Wendy and family , Auntie Linda , Auntie Carole , Auntie Sandra . The room seemed to be divided the rest of the motley crew were in the other part of the room. I sat looking at them all i saying to myself " you know what Angie you haven't missed a God dame thing and you never will.

After a couple of hours we said our goodbyes to those who we had been sitting with and to Lesley and the girls of course. Then we turned and left.

Stuart Owen Scaife aged 59 years .

Taken to soon.

25th july 1957- 22nd june 2017

May you rest in peace.

Chapter 9

We continued to go about our daily life , still enjoying our new home and meeting new people. Life was good and we were happy loving the right person is so rewarding to love and be loved felt wonderful.

Time flew by and before we knew it we were signing the lease for another year. We were so excited .

That was until the postman brought us a letter with news we didn't want to read it was news that had come out of the blue , well for me at least Michael had said he always knew that it would happen one day. Today turned out to be that day.

I opened the letter which looked very official which worried me straight away. I think i must have read it at least two or three times has i couldn't believe it.

I felt like the rug had just been pulled out from under my feet.

The letter was from the landladies Solicitor , yes the very same landlady who only a few days before stood drinking coffee with us , saying how much she loved what we had done with the place. I mean how two faced can you get?

We had been served a section 21 giving us just three months to find somewhere else to live and move out.

She had sold the place without even telling us. So once again i had to ring Michael at work with yet more bad news. When i read the letter out to him he said he wasn't at all surprised he had a feeling that she would do something like this. We were gutted .

When Michael got home he tried to ring her but she wasn't answering the phone to him. But after being persistent he finally got her to answer. He asked what was going on and why she didn't tell us that she was selling.

Her reply was that she was sorry but had to do it has she needed the money.

It was only afterwards that we found out she had done the same thing to the previous tenants. She had no intention of selling it. But to this day it is still standing empty which is mind boggling . Think of all the rent money she has lost doesn't make any sense at all.

Once we were over the shock of this the search began once again to find us a new home. It wasn't long before we found a lovely one bedroom bungalow this time in Cannock and it turned out to be just a ten minute walk from our friends Ric and Linda.

Hazel and Charlie were has gutted as we were that we were having to move but we had no choice.

We went to view the bungalow and we loved it , it is situated in a quite cul-de-sac. Having two large gardens that Michael really loved has he really does love to be out in the garden .

So that was it decision made we signed the papers and a moving in date was set. We were so happy to have found another home so quickly and so the packing began.

Within two weeks we were all moved out and moved into our new home. Yet again settling in the place was soon decorated, new carpets and Michael had worked his magic on both gardens , flowers planted , grass cut and reshaped if i say so myself it looked beautiful.

Everyone who passes by always comments on how lovely the garden looks which makes us feel very proud.

Chapter 10

It was just before we moved that i received yet another Official looking letter in the post. Before i opened it i thought what the hell can this be now?

Has i opened it i soon realized it was from another solicitor my heart missed a beat . But i need not of worried it was actually good news.

It seemed that my ex had filed for divorce and i was over the moon about that. But upon reading it i couldn't sign it and send it back.

The details were all wrong. I mean after 18 years of being married he had got my date of birth wrong even the details of the wedding date were completely wrong i did have to laugh at this i thought he must have got me mixed up with someone else. I mean stupid is as stupid does right???

Any way i sent the papers back un signed also agreeing to his terms which were that he was going to pay for the divorce if i didn't go after him for anything including money or his pension. But to be honest i just wanted rid of him as soon as possible. I wasn't interested in his money or anything else .

It was only a few weeks later that i again received another letter from the solicitor saying that the divorce had now been Finalised and i was now Offically divorced .

I cant tell you how happy that made me feel, i was actually free from him for good. I looked up to the sky and thanked God.

Chapter 11

It was now 2019. Michael and i had been together four years now. I must admit it was the happiest four years ever.

People never believed us when we said that we had never had a cross word, never had an argument , not one disagreement, he had never shouted at me, never made me cry.

He had made me laugh though so very much in fact we go to bed laughing and wake up laughing. The more time we spent together the more we learnt about each other and the more we discovered just how much we have in common.

From food to drink, from music to dancing, we have the same sense of humour and a very similar up bringing .. We both had had a tuff childhood but i suppose that is partly why we have turned out the way we have.

We love to have family and friends round for food and drink.Michael usually does the cooking while i make sure everyone has a drink in there hand.

Life is good and we cant complain.

Then one day Michael asked me the question , yes the question, he asked would i marry him??

Now this was something we had talked about a lot. On one occasion during a leap year i had actually text him while he was at work asking would he marry me? He was more than happy to say yes. That text is something we still laugh about to this day. So when he asked me face to face of course i said yes it would be a honour to be his wife. There were no words to describe just how happy we were.

The minute i said yes he was straight on the phone to his very best mate Jan who had gotten married to Roz just the year before. He went onto tell him that we were getting married and would he be the best man?

Of course Jan was only to pleased for us and being asked to be best man he gladly excepted.

So a date was set August 31st 2019   at the Cannock Chase Civic Centre at four pm. The invitations were sent out, the flowers were sorted, the dress, the suit the cake was ordered which when it arrived i actually decorated myself and to say i was happy with it was an under statement.the reception venue was booked.

We didn't waste time in getting everything organised for the big day which was quickly approaching .

Then the next thing we knew the big day had arrived and so did Martin with his girlfriend Nat. Both looking very smart, Martin more nervous than me has he was going to give me away.

The flower girls looked wounderful and were full of excitement . The car pulled up outside it was Michaels 1966 Chevy Impala a truly beautiful classic car wearing her white ribbons dressed for the occasion. She nearly out did the bride.

Everyone invited turned up the place was full to the brim. My dearest old school friend Grace was there smiling at me has i walked towards Micheal. He was looking so handsome and smart. Good enough to marry.

The day was just perfect it really couldn't have gone any better . Having a chance to see everyone and catch up with them all was wounderful and to see Grace there was brilliant it gave us a chance to have some up to date photos taken.

i must give a special thank you to Hazel and her daughter Charlotte and her other half for all the help and support they gave me, helping to decorate the room for the reception and to Charlotte for taking all the beautiful photos on the day it really was much appreciated.

Everyone enjoyed the day and night a goodtime was had by all or so i was told !!

Chapter 12

Married life was great, full of love and laughter. We were so happy together living our life.

Then all of a sudden the world changed .

A virus had hit the world big time . Covid 19 . It was said that it first started in a place called Wuhan in China. A pandemic something i never thought i would see in my life time. So many people were dying every day. Heart breaking wasn't the word. Sneezing , coughing, could so easily spread to others. Those that already had a underlining issuess were at a high risk of getting covid 19.

Although the situation was at its worse we didn't get put into lockdown until the march in 2020 that was when we were ordered to stay at home being allowed out only to get the essentials , food and medical things.

People were furloughed from there jobs. Meaning they couldn't go to work but they were allowed to work from home. We were told not to mix with anyone outside your home.

When we went shopping only one was allowed to go into the shop , keeping the risk of catching covid 19 down to a minimum . Face masks were worn hand Sanitiser was in place in the entrance of shops. Keeping your distance was another thing we were told to do.

We couldn't mix with family or friends. So text messages, voicemails, and of course video calls were the done thing just to keep in touch with family and friends.

On the plus side the weather was beautiful so that meant we spent a lot of time in the garden . Michael reshaping the garden , we had managed to get some bedding plants so we planted until our hearts were content.

For the evenings we entertained ourself . We would have house parties for two with food and music . We did make the most of the time together.

Watching the news on a daily bases was very depressing , people were dying every day, the hospitals were full to capacity, staff were ill and even dying, they didn't have the proper protective gear. They were truly over worked stretched to the limits and beyond.

Then for some unknown reason in June 2020 the restrictions were being eased, hence the covid cases began to rise yet again.

January 2021 arrived and we were put back into lockdown until July 2021.

People were slowly returning back to work, being told its ok to mix with family and friends once again. There was now a vaccine being offered , it became available in December 2020 and people were queuing up to have it.

But people were still catching Covid and still dying.

Michael and myself got Covid 19 just the once thank goodness it really knocked us off our feet but we nursed each other , looked after each other and after about a week we were well again.

Chapter 13

Being in lockdown sure did give you time to think about the days gone by . School days for example. I remember my first day at Homelands School on Village Street in Derby. I walked to school on my first day all alone. Carrying my school bag and wearing the uniform looking quite smart . White socks pulled up to my knees and shiney new shoes all brought with government vouchers. Mother had applied for them and was given the vouchers instead of money which was a good thing at least they couldn't spend it on booze and fags.

I arrived at the school gates and looking at the very long winding path i made my way up to the massive hallway. I wasn't sure how i found it but i did. From there i found the main hall where everyone had gathered, it was packed with new kids and the noise was so loud you couldn't really hear what anyone was saying.

I stood there looking around i didn't know anyone so yet again i was all alone feeling sick with nervous.

Then the head teacher arrived and the room fell quite. He called out names which formed a class then another teacher led us away to a classroom, and that was the day i met my first friend of the day. Dawn . She asked if she could sit next to me i said yes sure. When the first bell went for our first break of the day we spent it together .

Before we knew it we became really good friends .

Dawn lived on Wilin Street which was on my way home . We walked home together then i would carry on walking saying goodbye and i see you in the morning.

Sometimes i would have to go in to wait for Dawn in the mornings while her mum did her hair . Her mum and dad were always very kind to me. Dawn had a brother and a sister which made a lovely family. Her mum used to make me cheeses sand which with crusty bread followed by a cold glass of milk . I have to say they were the best cheese sand which i have ever had.

My other best friend came in the form of Grace . Grace lived on Clarence Road which was just about facing wilin street where Dawn lived.

Grace and i became really good friends . I loved going round to her house , her mum and dad were great and i always got a warm welcome.

Grace had had a baby boy so i also called for her on my way to school and we would take him to the nursery before going into .school. Once school was finished we would go and collect him and make our way back to Grace"s house. Where i would be offered a cold drink before going on way.

I remember Grace"s mum asked me to go round for my tea it was the day i had it really rough at home before heading off to school it was another bad time at home nothing had changed. I was still being picked on , hit and shouted at. I just couldn't do anything right at home so it was a relief being at school and out of the way. So when i was asked to go for tea i didn't need asking twice. I jumped at the offer and boy oh boy what a tea. It was more like a banquet i had never seen such a large table every inch of the table was covered in plates which in turn were covered in food chicken, rice and peas, plantin, and dumplings . Oh my God my eyes were bigger than my belly. There were glass jugs full of water or juice. I really hadnt seen anything like it but my goodness it sure was good , so tasty this is something i will always remember the kindness shown to me was unusal but i could have got used to it.

Graces mum always used to say that we were joined at the hip . Our friendship grew and Grace took me under her wings she looked out for me. She even let me sleep over at her house one night sharing her bed has i had ran away from home yet again.

Very sadly Grace has now lost her dad now and mum isnt in the best of health. But Grace works full time and still managers to look after her mum.

We still keep in touch al though we don't see much of each other now. Ive not seen her since she came to our wedding back in 2019 .. She hasn't changed a bit in fact she doesn't look any older and still has that same great smile.

Grace has always been with me in one way or another weather it be in her prayers or messages , sending me little cards with notes in them.She really is a true friend and I am proud to have her has a friend i thank her for being my true friend.

I also made other good friends while at Homelands. There was Denise who lived on Browning Street we used to go there during some break times and her mum always had the kettle on for us. Always had a welcome smile when i walked in.

In the summer break from school we used to meet up with Janetee and go either to Normanton Park on Warick Ave which was a lovely kept park , grass always cut and the flower beds were always planted and looked blooming lovely. Or we would go to Stenson fields well before they started building on it. We spent many a happy hour out there
.

All we had was a sandwich and a bottle of water we'd sit under the tree just chatting all day long trying to stay out of the sun because back in the 70s the summers were really hot proper summers , sunshine everyday it felt so good.

Denise and i remain friends to this day but unfortunatley we lost contact with Jeanette.

So really my school days at Homelands wasn't to bad.

Well that was until Wendy arrived . She to went to Homelands and boy did i know she was there. It wasn't long before she had got herself into bother with some lad.

I remember some kid coming running towards me shouting Angela , Angela its your Wendy shes in trouble. So me being me went running to find her just has the lad concerned hit her right across the face. I tried to get in the middle of them and just has i hit the lad back in his face the head teacher caught me.

I tried to explain what had happened but she wasn't having any of it i was marched off to her office where i was given two strokes of the cane across the tips of my fingers one for hitting the lad and one for answering her back.

Then Trevor joined us a tHomelands but he was quite and shy but he also had a fear of one of the teachers commonly known has Hitler . He wasn't a nice teacher i remember him throwing the blackboard cleaner at any one who he saw talking in class , he was also known for slapping you at the back of the head has he walked past you.

He did scare Trevor when he had a class with him poor little brother i used to just tell him to stay quite in class and keep his head down which i think he managed to do.

The more i thought about it the more i thought they would never get away with that sort of thing these days and that goes for our mother and father as well im pretty sure if they had treated us the way they did back then we would have been removed from the house it would be classed has child abuse now days.

These days i have no contact with mother i only ever see her at a family funeral and its then that i know for sure I haven't missed anything at all and neither have my children and my grandchildren.

I remember when Sarah and i went to see her in her flat that she now lives in. We were talking about father. So i ask her why didn't he like me? Why didn't he ever take to me?

What was it about me he didn't like? Her reply knocked the stuffing out of me. She said he didn't like you , never did he just ,couldn't take to you in fact he always thought you wasnt his. She added a a laugh which i thought was bizarre. Why would she think it was funny?

I just sat there with my mouth open i couldn't speak but when i found my voice again i said well i would never have guessed he had made it plain to me hated me and now i know why , he thought i wasn't his. I ask mother if i was and she told me of course of course i was but now the seed has been planted in my mind asking myself if he was my actual father after all he must have had a reason to think that in the first place. Sarah had put her arm around me saying Nanna you cant say things like that , nanna replyed why not its true and again laughed.

After that Sarah and i got our coats on and left . After that i don't think i ever went to see her again though i did used to phone her but to be quite blunt she wasn't intrested in me , my kids or my grandkids her only topic of conversation was our Dawn , our Dawn and if she mentioned Dawns son once she must have mentioned him a hundred times. Her front room was like a shrine to him.

So to me there was little point in going to see her, it was bad enough when i phoned her i could be on the phone to her for 10 minutes before she would say who is it anyway ? Has soon has she realised it was me she'd make an excuse to go. So that was that.

Trevor still rings her every two weeks but he says she is still the same , talks about Dawn Dawn and ho yeah Dawn . He does try with her and i have to say he is a better person than me . He never gets any recognition for everything that he does for her he does things in the shadow s but if it was Dawn she would shout it from the hill tops .so this is my chance to give Trevor a big shout out for being the kind person that you have become despite having such a tuff time growing up .

Chapter 14

Well what can i say about the year 2022.

It turned out to be the worst year ever. Just when you think everything in life is going great and nothing could upset you a bomb explodes right in the middle of your life.

It was to be the year that Michael and myself , family and friends would never for get. I was entering the ring for the biggest fight of my life . A fight that none of us knew who would come out the winner. The only thing i knew was i wasn't ready for it but left with no choice i had to go with the flow and come out fighting.

It was in July when i was called to attend my annual check up. I had a mammogram before i just remember it being painless but uncomfortable and it didn't take very long. So i wasn't really that worried about having it done.

I went along to the appointment at my local hospital . I was soon called in to start the procedure but for some unknown reason i knew something was wrong. The lady seem to be taking longer in one area. She went back again to the same spot .

Within two weeks i had got the letter i had been waiting for , the results had arrived but before i opened it i knew it wasn't going to be good news.

It said that i needed to have further investigations done my heart missed a beat and i looked at Michael . He took me in his arms and said everything was going to be alright. Try not to worry no matter what I am here for you, im not going anywhere .

So the waiting game began . The first appointment was in August to confirm that they had indeed found something in my right breast. I had a biopsy done and a marker inserted in the exact spot which was not a nice thing to have done but it needed doing and the nurses were so kind and caring they really tried to put me at ease which wasn't a easy thing to do.

While we waited on the results Michael was busy making plans for days away and long week ends away to take our minds off things.

We said we were not going to say anything to Sarah and the rest of the family until we knew what we were dealing with so it was our little secret for a short time. In the mean time Michael and myself talked about it and what might be happening but he kept reassuring me that i was going to be alright .

Finally on August the 19th the letter arrived with the news we didn't want to hear. I guess i already knew deep down. It confirmed that i had Breast Cancer it still came has a shock and i just couldn't believe it. The one thing i had always feared had got me .

We were advised to tell the family as soon as possible Michael held me in his arms telling me i was going to be ok , im not going anywhere, im here for you . He remained positive through out .

So then went we about telling the family. I rang Sarah to tell her that i had been having tests done and the result was breast cancer . She went quite for a second poor girl didn't know what to say. Michael was ringing his daughters and the response was much the same. No one knew what to say.

Sarah and Sam my eldest grandson came over i just hugged them both . There were a few tears but overall we had a good day. I told them everything and what was to come. I had been told that i would have to have chemo, radiotherapy and surgery and that I would loose my hair and all the other side effects were not going to be good. But i would just have to go with it and stay strong .they all were positive and reasuured me i will be ok. Sarah words to me were ' you got this mum'.

Sarah asked us to go over to see her on the following Friday so Michael booked a hotel and we spent that night with Sarah and her family . There was food , music and plenty of chat. We took photos of the family it was a great night. It was a good distraction it was much needed.

Our third wedding anniversary was just around the corner so Michael yet again booked a hotel in Telford he wined and dined me . He really is a kind caring man. We had a really good time although we still talked about my diagnosis .

Then the appointments started coming fast and furious. The first was on the 7th September for a for a CT Scan. The 8th September was for a Medical with Oncology nurses. It sure was a rough day but again i just went with the flow.

On the 22nd it was time to have a PIC line fitted which didn't really go to plan. I wasn't supposed to feel anything but i did it was so painful they had to take it out and try again this time it was ok , but it always gave me a problem in one way or another throughout the whole time. The PIC line was checked every week usually on a Monday along with blood tests.

We seemed to be spending more time at the hospital than we were at home. We soon got to know our way around the hospital. It was stressful and very tiring . But we both knew we had to find the energy from some where , we had to keep going.

My arm soon looked like a pin cushion and black with all the bruises .

My appointment to start chemo had now arrived . I was to attend New Cross Hospital on the 5th October at 12.15pm at the Snowdrop Department. It was another day we wouldn't forget.

Michael drove us to the hospital we chatted about anything and everything just to take our minds off the day ahead.

We arrived at the hospital and got out the car and the walk to the Department it seemed to take for ever although it was really only five minutes from the car park.

We got to the department where Michael had to leave me, he wasn't allowed to come in. He kissed me gave me a hug and said ' you got this darling' . I smiled took a deep breath and went through the doors. I didn't know what to expect . Michael had promised that he would be waiting for me when i got finished.

I walked through the double door walked up to the desk gave my name and was asked to take a seat.

After a short time my name was called and i could feel my heart beating. I stood up smiled and walked over to the nurse. She asked if i was alright yet again i gave a smile and yes thanks im fine. She weighed me , took my temperture it was then she took me into a side room and the doctor was called. My temperture was high and my heart beat was to fast.

They said i might not be able to go ahead today with the chemo.

I text Michael to tell him . We couldn't believe it , had i got myself worked up without knowning it?

But the doctor checked me over and after being sent for a x ray i was returned back to snowdrop where they decided i could start chemo after all they put it down to me being anxious. God knows how they thought i was feeling after all this was my first round of chemo i didn't know what was going to happen.

Then i was moved round to where the chemo was given . I sat in a chair and they began by putting a sickness bag via a drip into my PIC line that took an hour.

I was still texting Michael has he was waiting in the car
. It must have been worse for him has he coudnt see what
was going on , he relied on me keeping him updated.

Once the sickness fluid was finished the nurse brought a
black bag the Chemo ! She flushed the PIC line and the
chemo was inserted through my PIC line. So i drank water
and tried to relax. It took a few hours , the staff were all
very nice and caring coming round with the tea trolley and
offering sandwiches which i refused has i just could eat .

I managed to nod off for a few minutes , everyone having
treatment seemed to nod off at some point. There were quite
a few people having treatment and we all just smiled at each
other no one really talking except when the nurses spoke to
us.

Once the machine started to bleep indicating the
treatment had finished the nurse would flush the PIC line
once again put a dressing on it and i was told my next
appointment had been made for the following week.

I text Michael to say i was all done and i was on my way.
I walked out of the unit feeling so relieved it was over , i
opened the door and as promised Michael was standing
there waiting for me. I walked straight into his arms he
kissed me and asked if i was ok.

I remember saying actually i'm bloody hungry shall we
go for a carvery ? He laughed and said yeah come on lets
go.

While waiting for me Michael had been busy keeping
everyone updated on what was happening. Sarah had been
worried so he was chatting with her. Trevor had been
messaging him as well so everyone was being keep
informed .

I had been given a five day course of injections which
were to be injected into my tummy not something i thought

i could ever do to myself but just like everything else i had to do it and get used to it.

So the plan was in motion blood tests and PIC line check every Monday then if the blood test came back ok it would be chemo on Wednesday.

After my first round of chemo i didn't feel to bad in the first few days . Then all of a sudden it hit me i began to feel so tired i was finding it hard to stay awake. I felt sick but wasn't actually sick due to the sickness tablets i had been given to bring home with me.

I seemed to hurt all over . My head felt sore and the diarrhea kicked in. I just felt so unwell . There were times i had to have my blood tests re done has they had to be a certain level but my level kept dropping.

My consultant was keeping in touch with me via the phone or a cancer nurse would ring to see how i was getting on. I got phone calls from the oncology nurse as well to see how i was, every time i told them how i was they just said that's normal it the chemo.

But by the November i had a red rash which was all over my face, chest and neck. It was sore and i looked like a beetroot. The nurse had given me some cream and tablets.

I had lost all my hair by now no hair, no eye lashers, no eyebrows. My head was also sore from the chemo so i was told to put cream on it. I was having to wear hats all the time now even at night i wore a chemo cap as my head was so cold.

The side effects had kicked in well and truly. Not only did i feel like i had got cancer but even worse i looked like i had . And the feeling was heart breaking i had never ever thought this would happen to me. I started to think i was being punished for something but Michael told me i wasn't i was just very unlucky.

Poor Michael was having to do more or less everything i just couldn't muster up the energy to help. He even had to help me shower has i had to wear a PIC line cover and couldn't get it wet. He helped me to the toilet when i was really bad.

The nurse had told me to beef up a bit has i would need to be at a good weight to cope with the treatment. The only thing was i was finding it difficult to eat i just felt sick all the time and the smell of food didn't help. Michael would try cooking all sorts of different things trying to get me to eat.

I would manage a couple of mouth fulls but that was it i was full. I felt so guilty has Michael went to so much trouble to help me eat and i just couldn't do it.

I was drinking water like it was going out of fashion i couldn't even manage a coffee now normally i couldn't start the day without a coffee but now i struggled to drink it. The other thing i had gone off was chicken for some reason i just couldn't face it.

Michael was doing everything the washing, cleaning, cooking, even found time to keep the garden in good order . Gardening is his passion so it was his chance to go out and have his own space .

He took me to every appointment he never broke his promise that he had made me right in the beginning . He was there all the time for me twenty four seven nothing was to much bother for him . He really is my knight in shining armour.

It was hard on me not being able to see anyone because of my immune system being low. But it must have been hard for Michael as well . We had phone calls, text messages . Michaels phone was always going. Everyone would contact Michael incase i was sleeping or just not up to chatting.

Michael was still having to work when he could after all the bills still needed to be paid. When he did go to work he left me with strict instructions not to do anything and rest up.

Im sure there must have been times when he wanted to scream and shout or even have a good cry but he never did. He only showed me love and compassion the whole way through this nightmare.

So the chemo continued so did the side effects. The appointments were still coming it was all very stressful and so tiring.

My PIC line was still hurting , it wouldn't flush properly, and sometimes they couldn't get blood out of it. I bloody well hated that PIC line. It was sore and my arm was going red around where it was. So the team decided to do a swab to see if there was an infection there but it came back negative. The doctor had looked at it to see if it moved but they were happy with it saying it was still in the right place.

My arm was still hurting no matter what i did to try and soothe it. My head was still sore and i got head aches so i hit the paracetomol which gave a little bit of relief.

I spent my days either asleep or looking out of the window to see what was happening in the outside world. I was only going out when i had to go to the hospital and then i would come straight home. The ladies over the road would see me in the window and come over for a quick chat i'd open the window so i could hear them. They were the only ones in the road that knew i was unwell.

So now its mid December and im feeling rubbish but i had to keep going, hospital appointment came through to see the surgeon who was going to preform the operation once i had finished chemo and the radiotherpy treatment .

I knew i had still got along way to go. The journey was long and harsh and brutal.but i had to keep going i just had to.

I returned from a hospital appointment to find that Sarah was waiting for me i was shocked i really wasn't expecting to see her sitting on the sofa. I filled up had a quick hug and a chat but she couldn't stay long but it didn't matter it was so good to see her. Michael and Sarah had planned it and i thank them both for it. It really made my day.

My face, neck and chest was still very red and sore the nurses said it was a reaction to the chemo . I   was still looking like a beetroot and it was warm to the touch.

When i went to see my Consultant just before Christmas he didn't like the look of it so he cancelled the last two rounds of chemo saying it wouldn't make any difference has i had nearly finished this round of chemo and my skin needed time to repair its self before the other treatments could begin.

Christmas   came and Michael had gone above and beyond as usual . I tried to put the tree up but it took me so long has i had to keep stopping , i was really worn out but i wasn't going to let it beat me i kept on and finally did it.

Michael did all the Christams shopping, cooking and washing up bless him he really gave it one hundred percent. Just has he does in everything. He truly is a star.

On the 30th December i had to have a Ultrsound scan to check any changes ..

It wasn't all good news . It hadnt spread that was the good news but it hadnt shrunk either it had remained the same size so really i should have been grateful for that but i couldn't help feeling dissapointed i thought I had been through chemo once a week for 16 weeks and it hadnt done what i was hoping it would do.

I could feel my eyes watering so i took a deep breath , Michael took my hand and we went back to car i just wanted to go home.

I was still having my PIC line checked every week along with having blood tests done. The doctor had to have another look at it to make sure it hadnt moved . I was told it hadnt moved and it was fine. But i couldn't understand why it was so painful all the time.

In the mean time i was having to inject myself in my tummy twice a day but this caused brusing all over it was so so sore inside felt like it was on fire , the pain was becoming more and more unbearable . I just couldn't move without it hurting it made it hard to sit down , stand up , to sleep at night. The pain was waking me up when i did actually go to sleep. My tummy was swelling all the time it was starting to look like i had a rugby ball in there.

On January 23rd i was starting my next round of chemo only this time it was a cyclone red in colour . It didn't take has long to do but the side effects were the same .

The nurse that was looking after me in the unit was great she stayed by my side the whole time chatting away to me and told me everything she was doing. I was once again given tablets to take home and was told to carry on with the injections. Where i was supposed to inject i didn't know i had simply run out of room to inject.

After a few days i didn't feel right i felt so poorly. My pee was red and so was my face , my mouth was sore which made it hard to clean my teeth . The nurse had given me a mouth wash to help soothe it.

My bloods were low once again they kept dipping. Which made me feel even more tired i was still red it didn't seem to be getting any better, and i had now developed bone pain and boy it was painful . I remember thinking what else is going to happen was i being punished for something.?

71

My whole body was hurting just aching permanently it was hard to sit , stand , bend just about to do anything really.

My bloods remained to be low which explained why i was even more tired it was starting to feel overrwhelming .

My heart rate was still to fast so off i went again for another TheECG they just couldn't say why it was so fast.

I was beginning to feel really poorly by now. I remember my eyes were hurting i had dots and lines across my vision. Headaches and dizzy spells when i stood up, feeling sick and my legs were like jelly.

All i wanted to do was sleep..

My appointment was due to have my PIC line tested and my blood test. I got there not feeling well at all, when i arrived the nurse takes my temperture and asked if i was ok? For some reason i said yes im fine but i wasn't. She asked me to take a seat has i did so she fetched another nurse who the repeated my temperture it was 37.1 which was high . They asked me to follow them through to triage where i was examined by the doctor. Before i knew what was happing i had a candela inserted into my left hand, a drip had been put up and i was told to phone Michael and ask him to come as soon as possble. Lucky he was still in the car waiting for me , he came running up the stairs and was in with me within a minute. He found me all wired up and very nearly in tears because i just didn't realize what was going on.

They told Michael that i was going to have to be admitted has i was very poorly , all my vitals had crashed , they wouldn't even allow me to go home and pack a bag they said it was to dangerous.

Michael looked so worried i sat there in tears . He really doesn't like hospitals so he was being brave putting me first has he always does bless him .

When they had sorted me out Michael went home to fetch me my things but also informed Sarah what was going on he'd messaged Martin and Trevor .

While Michael was away i had more tests done . Michael returned with my over night bag a a supply of bottled water for me. He looked worried sick but still kept up beat telling me i was going to be alright and it wouldn't be for long i'd be home soon.

After he left i was taken to a ward , in the bay were three other ladies all very nice and chatty but i wasn't really in the mood for chat i just wanted to go to sleep but that wasn't going to happen anytime soon..

There were more tests to be done. Blood tests, wee tests, blood pressure , temperture and question after question . I knew it was for my own good but i really just needed to sleep.

I kept Michael updated as much as i could. Then in turn he would update Sarah , Martin, Trevor.

I was feeling worse by the minute , my temperture was still rising so i wasn't allowed a blanket , they placed a air conditioner right in front of me to try to get my temperture down but at the same time i was so cold inside.

A nurse took my chemo cap off and ran it under the cold water before putting it back on my head.

They said i was spiking , my breathing was shallow and heart rate was to fast for someone supposed to be resting. The doctor was called , who came and checked me over . More blood was taken .

This was repeated all through the night.

I tried to keep Michael posted on what was happing but there were times i forgot i'd just keep nodding off to sleep .

After a few days and all the results were back they were no nearer to finding out what was wrong with me all i knew was that i was getting worse , i didn't even know what day of the week it was or how long i had been there. It was Michael who told me i had been in hospital for nearly a week i couldn't believe it.

In the mean time i was doing my best to do something i'd force myself out of bed to go to the toilet , have a wash, change my clothes but it was really hard to do . I was drained it took everything i had to make it back to my bed.

Sarah and Sam had gone to see Michael at home and then all three came to see me at the hospital all looking so worried and started asking questions.

By this time i was on oxygen to help me breath and get my level back up. When Michael saw this he was so concerned he ask to see the doctor. He wanted to know what was going on but it seemed no one knew what was wrong with me.

He continued to ask about all the tests that i had wanting to know what the results were. After all i had been there a long time had x rays, scans, MRI. C T Scans but still nothing was showing up.

I was so poorly i can only just remember Sarah and Sam coming in to see me. A few days after that Martin came into see me he was looking worried but still smiled at me. He wanted to know what was going on and what all the tests were for and what the results were.

After nearly two weeks in hospital i couldnt remember anything , i was confused and kept forgetting what i was saying half way through or just forgot what i was going to say. I couldn't retain anything that was being said.

Then my doctor came to see me again. This time with some answers. I had to ask her to phone Michael has i was struggling to hear and understand her.

She was happy to ring Michael , which she did. But the phone call took Michael by surprise he wasn't expecting to hear a doctor on the other end of the phone. She went on to tell him that i had Septice, two blood clots on my lungs and also contracted legionnaires disease.

Wow what a list of things wrong with me. I cant help thinking why it took so long to find this out after all i must have had every test going .

So now i was started on Antibioctics straight away the drip was up and the antibiotics were given twice a daily also given by mouth twice a day . Michael came into see me and couldn't believe the difference just 24 hours on the right medication and i was sitting up talking and feeling hungry.

I was feeling so much better but i wasn't aloud to go home for another seven days has i had to finish the course of antibiotics and my temperture had to stay the same for three days. So the test carried on more blood test, another ecg , x rays, temperture checks every half an hour.

My appitite was slowly returning but to be honest the food wasn't really up to much. I found it really hard to eat anything they served up it was only just warm, sometimes i was finding hard to recognize what it was supposed to be.

But Michael once again came to my rescue bring me Greggs sausage roll, cakes sand which and i was drinking plenty of water. Even the coffee they gave us was just luke warm. But at least i was trying to eat something. Plus i was beginning to feel more like me again. Which i was feeling very thankful for.

Chapter 15

So after spending four weeks in the hospital where i had seen and heard some very sad things but also some happy things. I had been there when the nurses went on strike and boy was it different . Our ward had minimum staff and it was so quite. The staff that were there were run off there feet . They must have been so tired by the end of there shift, it was tiring watching them. But the still did the job with care and compassion. The cleaners with a cheerie morning smile making jokes making you laugh even if you didn't feel like it. What a ray of sunshine they were. Even the ladies that got to know me from the blood bank who would come so early in the mornings to yet again take more blood from me they were kind, gentle and caring. The other patients who chatted to me but also got to know if one of us were having a bad day just to leave us alone but giving a reassuring smile that was all that was needed. My doctor was lovely i remember one day i was feeling very tearful and has she was walking past me she stopped in her tracks and came over to me asking if i was ok? I really didn't know why i was feeling tearful that day but she sat down held my hand and sat chatting to me. When she went i was left feeling somewhat reassured. When Michael came to visit me it made me realise just how much i was missing him so when it was time for him to go he would phone me and tell me to look out of the window which my bed was next to. I looked out and there he was waving to me he had parked the car in front of my window i smiled so we chatted and waved to each other which got the attention of the lady next to me so she came to the window and waved back at Michael we did laugh. From then on we were called Romeo and Juliet . Everyone looked forward to Michaels visit has they said he was a ray of sunshine when he arrived we were greeted with a good afternoon ladies how are we today ? With that big smile of his. He really did cheer us all up.

I had seen patients come and go but wondered when would it be my turn to be discharged . I just wanted to go home.

At last i was finally told that once my antibiotics were finished i would be well enough to go home which was the following Saturday i couldn't wait. The day finally arrived at 11am on the dot Michael was there and i had been sitting waiting since 6am excited to be going home at last . Four weeks in hospital was such a long time and now it was my turn to be discharged. I said my goodbyes to my fellow paitents and to the nurse's who had cared for me , one nurse inparticular came to say goodbye and wished me well she gave me a hug and that was it i was off. I will be forever grateful to the NHS has we got to the car i looked up to the window where i had stood waving to Michael on many occassions only to see my friend from the next bed to me waving . I smiled up at her and gave her a big wave before getting into the car.

At last i was on my way home i looked at Michael and he was just as happy has i was . We arrived home the first thing i did was give Michael a massive hug and thanked him for being there for me. Then i went and had a long hot shower now that my PIC line had been removed while i was in hospital i didn't have to worry about it getting wet. Michael had told Sarah that i was now at home and she was so very pleased has was Martin and Trevor. The very next day Trevor and Lisa came to see me and it sure was good to see them it had been to long.

Chapter 16

So the tests continued . On may 27th 2023 i went for my pre op assement ready for the operation which was June 1st. I was to be on the ward for 7am that day, which i was . Michael yet again having to wait outside. It was a very long day for us both. After having more tests i was taken to the operating theatre for the surgeon to remove the cancer it took over two hours but the next thing i remember was waking up in the recovery room. The operation had gone well and after being checked over i was discharged the same day , home by 6.30pm. I was now in the recovery period at home walking around in my not so sexy surgical stockings which i had to wear for three weeks. I was still attending my appointments with my consultant which went well he seemed happy with my progress. Since i was well enough i was given a course of chemo tablets to start . Twice a day for two weeks then a week of resting then start over again this went on for another three months. They had side effects but after what i had been through i knew i could cope with it. While i was having this treatment i was admitted once again to hospital this time for the large haematomia that had developed in my tummy due to the injections it was so painful and it felt like it was burning inside me. After more scans and examinations by the doctors i was allowed home the next day with more painkillers.

In August i had my first zoneta treatment (bone repair) which is to help repair the damage done by the chemo to my bones. This is to be repeated twice a year for the next three years. There are side effects to this as well but i seemed to have coped with it this time. Fingers crossed it continues. It is administered via a drip in the arm and takes about an hour. Its not very nice but its another thing i have

to do. In between this i was still attending appointments ,
having blood tests done on a regular bases.

My appointment to start the radiotherapy had arrived and
i was to start on the 7th September for a five day course. It
went well and again there was to be side effects which i
coped quite well with. So i am now edging towards the end
of my chemo tablets but still feeling the effects from them
, but slowly im feeling a little better getting back to my old
self. My hair was starting to grow back which i was over
the moon about , so to were my eyebrows and eye lashers i
was even starting to look like me again. Although my skin
was still slightly red it wasn't so sore.

I have now been told that the cancer had completley gone
and i am now in in remission . It had been a long brutal,
harsh painful jounery one that i wouldn't wish on anyone.
Its now time for me to start living my life again and live it
to the fullest. 2024 is going to be full of catching up with
family and friends which i am so very lucky to have. I'll be
going out places and of course have a hoilday which is
something we have not been able to do for some time what
with covid and then my illness.

Before i go i just want to say a massive thank you to the
NHS You have shown nothing but kindness, support, and
caring with such compassion during what has been the most
horrendous time of my life i will be for ever grateful.

To Sarah and Guy and all three of my wounderful
grandsons for all your support , kindness and encourgement
, for being there for me all the positivity you surrounded me
with. You were not just there for me but you showed your
kindness to Michael (pops) as well.

Michael Decosta…….. Not only are you my husband
but you are my best friend . You never broke the promise
you made to me at the beginnig of this jounery . You always
went above and beyond in everything you did and still carry
on doing for me. You have lived every minute of this with

me and for that i will be forever grateful. You have shown me so much love, treated me with kindness and respect and compassion. Nothing has fazed you through out this , you have been so brave and strong .

Thank you doesn't seem enough for everything you did and continue to do. As we try to get back to some sort of normality we can pick up where we left off living our life and live it we will to the fullest .

We hope and prey that my good health continues for many more years to come we can now enjoy our new found happiness.

To all my family and friends that were there for me when i needed you i thank you from the bottom of my heart.

I couldn't have done it without any of you.

To those that have read my story and may be going through the same thing i say to you stay strong stay positive and just go with the flow. And remember what my daughter said to me time and time again.   YOU GOT THIS.

Milton Keynes UK
Ingram Content Group UK Ltd.
UKHW052313020724
445051UK00046BA/1357